Preface

With a little encouragement from the Goodhue County Historical Society, it didn't take me long to want to do research on Frontenac Station. This once thriving little village is located eleven miles from Red Wing and about eight miles from Lake City. Earlier their main street, which ran parallel with the Milwaukee, Chicago, & St. Paul Railroad line, was Columbia Street, which later became US Highway 3 and eventually US Highway 61.

A lot of information has been written about its neighbor, Old Frontenac, or as the residents call it today, Old Town, but New Frontenac, as many have called it over the years, or as the sign says as you enter the town, Frontenac Station, has had very little recognition.

As I started my research, I stopped at the local restaurant, The Whistle Stop, and told many of the local residents who were customers that day, that I was starting to do research about their town, which would later be made into a book, and that I would need their help. They were so excited; they began recalling stories and information.

The locations of a few of the businesses were already well known, but some businesses I placed in the book according to pictures, newspapers, and abstract information. The locations of some of the original businesses are still unknown and will need further research.

I decided also to mention various points of interest within a few miles of Frontenac Station, such as various mills, elevators, the Lake City Airport, the former community of Pleasant Valley, Bramble Haw, school districts 24, 25, 26, and 27, and the village of Florence.

I do apologize for errors that occurred while putting this information together. Basically, it is my interpretation as to where some businesses locations and the construction of the information, as I saw it, may vary from others' perspectives. Quotations and submitted materials have been edited for consistency and clarity.

Acknowledgments

This book was written with the cooperation and assistance of the Florence Township History Center, in association with Friends of the Florence Town Hall. A special thanks to Evelyn Kiester, Judy Johnson, Sylvia Smythurst, and Virginia Oliver, members of the Friends of the Florence Town Hall, for their cooperation, help, and faith in an amateur researcher, to do this enormous task of researching Frontenac Station.

I especially want to thank former staff member Diane Buganski and staff member Johanna Grothe of the Goodhue County Historical Society, for suggesting this project and for their assistance in helping create this book.

Photo Credits

The author wishes to thank the Goodhue County Historical Society, the Florence Township History Center, and the many individuals who generously donated information, photos, and personal family pictures.

I also want to thank the following people who have contributed information and photos used in this book: "Butch" Berlin, Shirley Sommerfield, Bertha Neiderhouser, Carol Davidson, Naomi Roper, Marshall Laidlaw, Victor Wiech, Marjorie Dunbar, Laura Stemper, Michael Murphy, Robert Parrott, Pat Possehl, Marcia Savela, Judy Huneke, Mrs. Arland Adler, Gary Schumacher, Syvilla Bloom, Ellen Stewart, Ken Hoffman, Judy Steffenhagen, Andru Peters, Pastor Paul Otto, Vance Cushing, Barbara Hanson, Caroline Earhart, Norma Nemeth, Jean Dankers, Lorna (McKeen) Podvin, William Laidlaw and Jennifer Stauffer.

Editing

Char Henn

Design and Production

Wendy Amundson

Printing

ISBN 978-1502482341

© 2014 by Sharon Nelson

Table of Contents

Acknowledgments 2

Plat Map of Frontenac Station 1894 4

Frontenac Station 5

Depot at Frontenac 11

Post Offices 17

Frontenac State Bank 21

St. John's Lutheran Church 23

The Creameries 31

Florence Town Hall and Town Hall Events 36

General Merchandise, Dry Goods, and Grocery Stores 46

Restaurants 74

Service Stations, Garages, and Auto Repair Shops 82

Taverns, Bars, and Saloons 92

The Frontenac Ice Company and Stockyards 115

The Local News 125

The Elevators 134

Frontenac Stone Company 139

Various Mills in Florence Township 147

Blacksmiths 154

Early Residents 156

Goodhue County Abstract Office Information 199

The Village of Florence 204

Florence Township Schools 24, 25, 26, and 27 207

Bramble Haw 214

The Lake City Airport 217

Plat Map of Frontenac Station (1894)

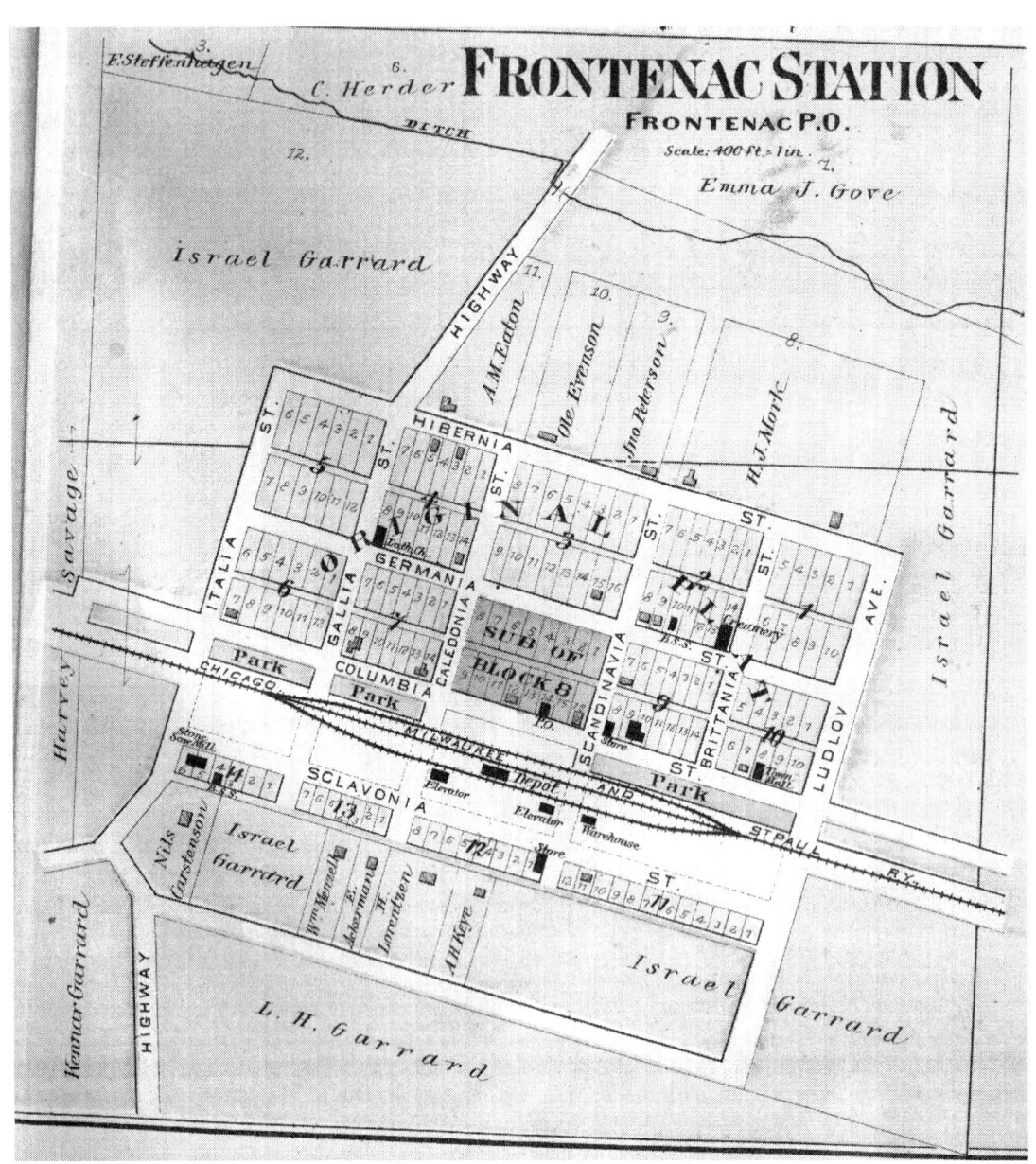

(GCHS)

US State Highway 3 heading east toward Frontenac Station. (GCHS)

In 1921 the old military road became US State Highway 3 and by 1934 it had changed to US State Highway 61. US Trunk 61, in the old system, followed Minnesota Trunk 3, from La Crosse to the Twin Cities, and Highway 1 from there to Canada. In the new system US State Highway 61 carries no number but its own.

A view of US Highway 3, railroad tracks and an elevator as you enter Frontenac Station, ca. 1911.

Frontenac Station

View of Frontenac Station, taken from Waconia Bluff in the 1880s (Photo courtesy of Ellen Stewart and the Hodgson family)

Frontenac Station

Florence Township was established in 1858 and was named Florence in honor of Florence Graham, daughter of Hon. Christopher C. Graham, a receiver in the land office and justice of the peace in Red Wing.

Frontenac Station is located next to the Chicago, Milwaukee & St. Paul Railroad (Milwaukee Road) line, about eleven miles southeast of Red Wing on US Highway 61 and eight miles northwest of Lake City.

In 1871 agents from the Chicago, Milwaukee & St. Paul Railroad wanted to build the railroad line through Old Frontenac and approached Israel Garrard about acquiring property. Refusing to sell them land because he wanted to preserve the quiet, commercial-free atmosphere of Old Frontenac, he donated land two miles south of Old Frontenac for the new railroad line. Shortly after the railroad was built through the area in 1871, the village of Frontenac Station was platted and was the last village to be established in the area.

Frontenac Station consisted of eight square blocks, with the following street names—Germania, Italia, Britannia, Hibernia, and Scandinavia streets and Ludlov (Ludlow) Avenue, which was named for the maternal branch of the Garrard family. The main street, known as Columbia, ran parallel with the railroad, with a small business district established on the north side of the street. Later Columbia Street became US State Highway 3 and eventually US State Highway 61. Sclavonia Street, located on the south side of the village one block south of the Chicago, Milwaukee and St. Paul railroad, housed more early businesses.

By 1878 Frontenac Station was a fast-growing little community, with a depot, three stores, three blacksmith shops, a grain elevator, and a population of one hundred. Later, saloons, a creamery and cheese factory, a stone sawmill, a lumber mill, a service garage, a bank and a hotel were established. Frontenac Station was a bustling little village with Florence Township residents bringing their crops to town for shipment by rail.

By the 1950s truck transportation made it easier for farmers to take their products to larger grain elevators in neighboring towns, and soon some of Frontenac's businesses were beginning to disappear.

Today this quiet little community is left with very few businesses and most people who live there are retired or commute to work in larger cities nearby. Yet today there are still people living in Old Frontenac and Frontenac Station who can proudly say that they are descendants of some of the early settlers that made these two villages and the surrounding area their home.

H. Lorentzen's Frontenac Cash Store, a general merchandise and provisions store, is shown in the center of the photo; next to the store was the residence of William and Nancy Herlinger, some of the first pioneer settlers in Florence Township. The depot is on the far left with a grain elevator on the far right. ca. 1873 (Photo courtesty of GCHS)

In 1870 the population of Florence Township was 768, with 154 families and 149 houses.

WACOUTA TOWNSHIP.

Name.	Residence.	Business.	Nativity.	Came to State	PostOffice
Peterson, Hans		Farmer & Stk Raiser	Denmark	1865	Red Wing.
Post, A. W.	Section 36	Farmer	Ontario Co., N. Y.	1853	"
Post, George	" 36	Farmer & Stk Raiser	Ontario Co., N. Y.	1855	"

FLORENCE TOWNSHIP.

Name.	Residence.	Business.	Nativity.	Came to State	PostOffice
Arnold, Wm. S.	Section 33	Farmer & St'k raiser	St. L'wr'nce Co. N Y	1858	Lake City.
Brown, W. B.	" 32	Farmer & St'k raiser	Chittenden Co., Vt.	1865	"
Brock, Jacob S.	" 21	Farmer & St'k raiser	Rensselaer Co. N.Y	1865	"
Bailey, H. W.	" 32	Farmer & Grain r's'r	Bennington Co. Vt.	1857	"
Bennewitz, John C	" 5	Farmer & Grain r's'r	Prussia	1856	Frontenac.
Carey, Maria	" 35	Farmer & St'k raiser	Fulton Co., N.Y.	1854	Lake City.
Doane, C. A.	" 36	Lumbering	Onondaga Co., N.Y.	1856	"
Eaton, Edwin C.	" 27	Farmer	Kent Co., England	1854	"
Francisco, O. P.	" 36	Farmer & St'k raiser	Hamilton Co., N.Y.	1856	"
Freeman, T. E.	" 24	Farmer	Wayne Co., Pa.	1856	"
Foss, Joel N.	" 32	Farmer & St'k raiser	Rockingham, N. H.	1857	"
Garrard, Israel	Frontenac	Farmer	Cincinnati, Ohio	1854	Frontenac.
Herlinger, Wm. G.	Section 14	Farmer & Hotel kpr.	Northampton, Pa.	1855	Fronten.Sta.
Holliday, John	" 33	Farmer	Scotland	1861	Lake City.
Kelly, Moses C.	" 24	Farmer & St'k raiser	Holmes Co., Ohio	1853	"
Keye, A.	" 17	Farmer & St'k raiser	Germany	1856	Frontenac.
Loventzen, H.	Fronten.Sta.	Gr'n dlr. & Gen. Mdse Farmer & St'k r's'r	Hamburg, Germ'y.	1856	Fronten.Sta.
Lewis, Eli N.	Section 8	Farmer & St'k raiser	Pennsylvania	1854	Frontenac.
Longsdorf, Jno. H.	" 34	Farmer	Cumberland Co. Pa	1864	Lake City.
McNeil, H.	" 34	Farmer	Saratoga Co., N.Y.	1864	"
Murray, G. C.	" 13	Milling	Michigan	1871	Fronten.Sta.
Morrison, James	" 18	Farmer & St'k raiser	Quebec, Canada E.	1865	Frontenac.
Miller, John	" 30	Farmer	Switzerland	1864	"
Munger, J. C.	" 25	Farmer & St'k raiser	Van Buren, Mich.	1855	Lake City.
Merrill, Truman D	" 24	Farmer	Otsego Co., N.Y.	1854	"
Munger, Eliab	" 14	Farmer & St'k raiser	Van Buren, Mich.	1855	Frontenac.
Nute, John	" 36	Farmer & St'k raiser	Carroll Co., N. H.	1866	Lake City.
Potter, Calvin		Farmer	Pennsylvania	1852	Red Wing.
Reed, Mrs. Calfine	" 36	Farmer	Ontario Co., N.Y.	1864	Lake City.
Sutherland, James	" 6	Farmer	Dutchess Co., N.Y.	1858	Red Wing.
Schneider, J.	Fronten.Sta.	Grocer	Germany	1858	Fronten.Sta.
Starr, Harriet A.	Section 35	Farmer	Cayuga Co., N.Y.	1856	Lake City.
Stroup, Wm.	" 28	Farmer & St'k raiser	Oneida Co., N.Y.	1866	"
Skinner, Luzon	" 24	Farmer	Wayne Co., N.Y.	1854	"
Thomson, John	" 21	Farmer & St'k raiser	Scotland	1863	"
Vining, David H.	" 23	Farmer & St'k raiser	Greene Co., N.Y.	1855	"
Vining, E. M.	" 23	Farmer	Pike Co., Pa.	1855	"
Westervelt, E.	Fronten.Sta.	Farmer	Duchess Co., N.Y.	1852	Fronten.Sta.
Wrigley, Edwin	Section 35	Farmer & St'k raiser	England	1855	Lake City.
White, Joel	" 32	Farmer	Providence, N. B.	1865	"

Frontenac Station ca.1910. Looking from left to right: the Albert Schmidt house, the White Store, center, with L. C. Tackaberry's house next door. The depot is across Columbia Street, with the grain elevator on the far right behind the depot. (Photo courtesy of Florence Township History Center) GCHS

A bird's-eye view of Frontenac Station, ca. 1910. The Frontenac elevator is on the far left of the photo, while on the north side of Columbia Street, on the far left, is a one-story house, which is now the two-story residence of David and Shirley Sommerfield. St. John's Church is in the background. In the center was Albert Schmidt's large two-story house, with the White Store and depot on the right.

The depot at Frontenac with grain elevator, warehouse, feed mill, and storage sheds (Photo courtesy of Barbara Hanson)

The Milwaukee depot, with the White Store, and L. C. Tackaberry's house on the right. (Photo courtesy of Ellen Stewart and the Hodgson family)

Depot at Frontenac

(Photo courtesy of GCHS)

The Milwaukee Depot at Frontenac

By 1871 the building of Chicago, Milwaukee & St. Paul railroad tracks had been completed between Lake City and Red Wing.

In July 1871 the depot at Frontenac was completed except for painting and was dedicated by a dance and a good time by many people from Lake City and Red Wing. (1871 Lake City *Graphic-Republican*)

The depot was a wood-frame building with two entrances. One end was used as a waiting room for passengers and the other end was for baggage and freight handling. There was a stationmaster, a telegrapher, and someone to take care of the freight at the depot daily. The Western Union Telegraph Company was also located within the depot.

Albert Keye, telegrapher at the Milwaukee Depot. (GCHS)

There were several station agents over the years, including C. F. Dodge in August 1871 (according to the 1871 Lake City *Sentinel*). In 1880 George H. Dodge was the station agent and A. E. Hazzard came in 1882, but left that year to become depot agent at Minneiska. The following agent came from River Junction. O. K. Anderson was the agent from 1885 to 1887, and

Depot at Frontenac

Frank B. Lister, formerly the night operator at Lake City, had been appointed station agent in 1887, followed by Mr. Eckert. J. H. Mues was the station agent for a number of years until he retired in 1894, and in 1898 M. P. Peterson was the station agent of the Milwaukee Company at Frontenac Station.

In 1898 the first train service began stopping at Frontenac Station twice a day bringing the mail. With the large number of passengers arriving and departing at Frontenac Station to spend time at the Lakeside Hotel in Old Frontenac, the passengers requested that this accommodation be provided. This lasted until 1912, when the eastbound Milwaukee train stopped at Frontenac Station only when tickets were sold.

Milwaukee Depot. (Photo courtesy of GCHS)

Receipts had dropped from $10,000 in 1927 to $4,000 in 1931. The following year the railroad proposed the elimination of the station agent and substitution of custodian service for Frontenac Station. They petitioned the state commission for permission to make Frontenac Station a custodian station. This would mean that tickets would not be available and freight or express shipments could not be made under this plan. Trains #55 and #58 would still stop at this station, but the telegraph office would be discontinued under this plan. This would have meant a huge loss for the community of Frontenac Station. Thankfully that the plan did not go through, but eventually, with the growing popularity of automobiles and the competition from truck transportation, there was little need for trains to stop at Frontenac Station. Having outlived its usefulness, the depot closed in 1971 and was removed after 1976.

Depot at Frontenac

The Depot News

H. Lorentzen, postmaster at Frontenac, was seriously injured on Monday, while standing on the depot platform at that place, by being struck by a mail sack as it was thrown from a train, running at the rate of forty miles an hour.

(April 1891 The Advance Sun)

The post office and Milwaukee depot at Frontenac were broken into. Some cash was taken and express, parcel post, and freight packages were gone through. L. C. Tackaberry, postmaster and station agent, stated that about $3 in change was taken, and a box of candy was broken into and four bars of sweets were reported missing. Local sheriff and police were notified.

(1922)

The insulators are being put on the poles and communication by telegraph will be in operation between Frontenac Station and Russell & Son's mill soon.

(1882 Lake City Republican)

Lester (L. C.) Tackaberry, Postmaster, Station Agent, and Telegrapher
The depot at Frontenac is shown on the right, the White Store is on the far left, and the Tackaberry house is directly behind L. C. Tackaberry. (Photo courtesy of the Tackaberry family)

On January 15, 1915, Tackaberry was appointed to US postmaster at Frontenac Station. He also was the depot agent, and telegrapher for the railroad.

Depot at Frontenac

Roy Tackaberry was the son of Lester and Jeannette Tackaberry. Roy was not fond of the name Wilbur, so he always went by either Roy or "Tac." Roy worked for the railroad and was very savvy regarding railroad regulations and was a Morse code expert. He married Alice Louise Nelson and for some time they lived with Roy's parents. Alice served as acting postmaster in 1945 at Frontenac Station before she was married.

Roy Tackaberry standing in front of the depot at Frontenac Station with his Harley Davidson motorcycle, single, cylinder engine.

A special train for the J. I. Case Threshing Machine Company heading west, loaded with forty to fifty threshing outfits. The cars were decorated with flags and bunting. A huge crowd in Red Wing was waiting for this special train, ca. 1900 (April 28, 1900 Republican) (Photo courtesy of GCHS)

During this era, trains were also called "pufferbellies." (GCHS)

Steam engine which served as a portable wood cutting mill. (GCHS)

Depot at Frontenac

A rail crew in 1907. (Photo courtesy of GCHS)

Louis Wohlert and the rail crew. (Photo courtesy of the Wohlert family, submitted by Shirley Sommerfield)

Louis Wohlert moved to Frontenac in 1918 and worked for the Milwaukee Railroad until 1937. He moved to La Crosse, Wisconsin, but returned to Frontenac in 1956, when he retired from the railroad.

Westervelt Post Office 1855-1860
Old Frontenac

Evert Westervelt, a Pennsylvania carpenter and furniture maker, became the town's first postmaster, in the village called Westervelt, on May 9, 1855. The post office was believed to have been in his home.

The name of the village, along with that of the post office, was changed to Frontenac on January 18, 1860, with James Owens serving as its first postmaster, until 1862. That same year, the post office was moved to a small area within Jacob Schneider's, combination store/tavern. William E. Lowell would follow as postmaster, that same year, until 1864.

Frontenac Post Office
Various Locations

Earlier, Frontenac received its mail supply from Red Wing by stage, until the building of the Chicago, Milwaukee & St. Paul Railroad which then supplied the mail. According to Mrs. E. J. (Herlinger) Gove, in a booklet Historic Frontenac - Methodist Campus, she states: "our first post office was kept by Henry Lorentzen in our own home at Frontenac. After the railroad came through it was moved to the station". This put the first post office in Frontenac Station at the William and Nancy Herlinger house around 1872. Shortly after, the post office was moved to the Milwaukee depot. According to the 1894 plat map of Frontenac Station, the post office was then located on lot 14, in block 8. This put the post office at the home of Herman Scherf who was postmaster in 1893 until 1915. Lester Tackaberry then became post master and served from 1915 until 1945. A 1922 article stated that the post office and depot were broken into with cash taken. This put the post office back at the Milwaukee depot by 1922, until 1934.

Frontenac Post Office and former residences of Herman Scherf and L. C. Tackaberry.

Frontenac Post Office 1934-1945
Lester Tackaberry Residence

In January 1934, the Frontenac post office changed locations—from the Milwaukee depot to L. C. Tackaberry's house, which was located next door to The White Store or next to the present, Whistle Stop. The former Tackaberry house is still at this location, and according to Alice Tackaberry, the exterior of the house has not changed very much over the years.

Frontenac Post Office 1946-1947

Charlson's White Grocery

From 1946 to 1947, Mrs. Rudy (Maxine) Charlson housed the postal service in her store, Charlson's White Grocery.

Post Office located on the NW corner of Scandinavia and Germania Streets.

Waldo Bonde

United States Post Office 1947-1982

In 1945, while recuperating from injuries received in World War II and considering his physical limitations, Waldo Bonde decided to take a civil service exam, figuring a postmaster job might be a good career.

Passing the test, he had a job but no post office. At that time, the post office was being housed at The White Store, a grocery store up for sale, by its owners Rudy and Maxine Charlson, who was also acting postmaster at that time.

Bonde purchased a corner lot on the northwest corner of Germania and Scandinavia streets. After checking the Sears Roebuck catalog, he found a 12 x 20-foot prefabricated building, which came in sections. The prefab building arrived by train at Frontenac Station, where it was picked up and assembled by Bonde and Carl Springer. Bonde became postmaster in May of 1947 and served until 1974.

The office opened with forty-five post office boxes, and started out as a fourth-class post office with neither restroom nor a ramp for the handicapped. Headquarters wanted to see these two facilities in all post offices and, if residents chose to continue present operations, the building would have had to be upgraded or the service moved.

In 1947 a first-class stamp cost three cents. A small post office box was rented for sixty cents a year; a mid-size box cost one dollar. Mail used to be picked up and delivered by trains running between Chicago and the Twin Cities. Trucks replaced trains in the 1960s.

The tiny wooden building had not only been a post office but a meeting place for Frontenac residents for close to thirty-five years.

A move was made to close the post office in the mid-1960s. The attempt was met with opposition.

(January, 1982 Red Wing Republican Eagle article written by Debra Olson, staff writer)

FRONTENAC POST OFFICE
GOODHUE COUNTY, MINNESOTA

Name	Title	Date Appointed
(Originally established as WESTERVELT)		
Evert Westervelt	Postmaster	05/09/1855
Name changed to FRONTENAC on January 18, 1860		
Evert Westervelt	Postmaster	01/18/1860
James A. Owens	Postmaster	01/07/1862
William E. Lowell	Postmaster	08/19/1862
Henry Lorentzen	Postmaster	08/19/1864
Herman Scherf	Postmaster	04/15/1893
Lester C. Tackaberry	Postmaster	01/05/1915
Miss Alice Nelson	Acting Postmaster	07/31/1945
Mrs. L. Maxine Charlson	Acting Postmaster	05/31/1946
Waldo E. Bonde	Postmaster	05/16/1947
Alfred E. Eastlund	Officer-In-Charge	06/28/1974
Alfred E. Eastlund	Postmaster	09/14/1974
Jon B. Gravenish	Officer-In-Charge	01/11/1980
Donald F. Busch	Postmaster	05/31/1980
Pamela S. Gorman	Officer-In-Charge	10/30/1981
Randy L. Kahl	Officer-In-Charge	03/26/1982
Candace J. Marthaler	Postmaster	11/13/1982
John Bergin	Officer-In-Charge	01/04/1991
Rhonda J. Taylor	Postmaster	12/11/1993
Linda Newcomb	Officer-In-Charge	02/18/1999
Richard A. Schaar	Postmaster	05/08/1999
Debra Olsen	Officer-In-Charge	04/12/2001
Cindy R. Hinkel	Postmaster	06/02/2001
Al Walther	Officer-In-Charge	03/28/2005
Michael W. Wotrang	Postmaster	08/20/2005

Post Office 1984-2014

Frontenac Station

In 1920 George and Virginia Garrard sold lot 9 in block 10 to the town of Frontenac Station, for $150. This lot, next to the Florence Town Hall, would later house Frontenac Station's post office.

In 1983 the postal department was looking to move its Frontenac office. In 1984 the Florence town board and the postal department signed a lease whereby a trailer-type office, that was designed to be used as a post office, located next to the Florence Town Hall, would sit on the back of lot 9, with a blacktopped parking lot.

The post office had 110 post office boxes and 120 rural route customers, and was one of the smallest offices to employ a full-time postmaster. From 1987 to 1991 the post office showed a decline of office receipts. The government estimated that it could save about $27,000 a year by closing the office.

When small post offices lose a postmaster, postal officials routinely re-evaluate the role of the office to determine whether it should remain open. Revenue, the number of deliveries, and the population of the community are factors typically considered in deciding an office's fate.

About 1991, the US Postal Service figured this unincorporated village along US Highway 61, south of Red Wing, was nearly dead and began taking steps to close the post office and send its customers to nearby Lake City. If the office closed, Frontenac residents would most likely receive Lake City addresses. Local delivery would continue, but anyone requiring a post office box would have to drive to Red Wing or Lake City.

In 1993 the postal service wanted to consolidate the post office with an office in Lake City. This was the fourth time the US Postal Service had attempted to close or consolidate its Frontenac office.

(1993 Post-Bulletin)

The news outraged Frontenac residents, who argued that the Postal Service didn't have the facts straight. With the dedication of Doris Berlin, café owner, who got signatures of 174 residents, township leaders took their case to everyone that would listen. Frontenac Station took on the bureaucracy and won—the post office remained open.

John Schmauss, of Lake City, was president of the Frontenac State Bank, with Albert Schmidt, vice president, Kirk E. Hindman, cashier, and Irma Gercken, bookkeeper. (Photo courtesy of the Florence Township History Center)

Frontenac State Bank 1919-1931

The Frontenac State Bank was founded on August 28, 1919, by men prominent in the business and social life of the district, such as Anton Schafer, A. R. Santelman, John Alpers, Albert Schmidt and Fred Wohlers.

The home of the Frontenac State Bank, located on US State Highway 3, was one of the prettiest small bank structures in the state. It was 35 by 40 feet in dimension, stucco design and erected especially for use as a country bank. The bank was a member of the National and State Bankers Association.

The interior was attractively arranged with a lobby, customers room, director's chamber, and banking cages. The interior finish being of solid oak, in a golden finish. The latest design of Diebold Safe & Lock Co. bank vault was installed.

In 1924 the present capital stock of the bank was $15,000, and a surplus of $3,000 was carried. The resources of the bank totaled $108,000 and carried $80,000 in deposits, of which $15,000 was placed in savings deposits, with an interest rate of 4 per cent, being paid.

Kirk E. Hindman, the new cashier, was a young man with sixteen years of varied and broadening experience along banking lines. It was in 1908 that he first started with the First Security State Bank of Red Wing. He left there eight years later to work for the Union Bank of Canada, at Winnipeg, where he remained two and a half years. After nine months in the war service and a year as deputy examiner with the Minnesota State Banking Department, he took his present position in September, shortly after the Frontenac State Bank opened its doors for business.

(1924 Lake City Graphic-Republican)

Through its practice of making loans to deserving persons, which provided capital to carry on business, whether farming, dairying, stock raising, or mercantile, and by discounting certain classes of negotiable paper, the Frontenac State Bank was a powerful partner for every legitimate business enterprise of the community.

When Cashier Hindman came to work one day in 1927, he found that robbers had made an attempt to open the bank door by burning a hole with an acetylene torch, but a safety device inside prevented this and the robbers failed.

Following the stock market crash of 1929, public confidence in banks was shaken and many customers started to withdraw their money. On October 22, 1931, the board of directors of the Citizens Bank of Lake City and the Frontenac State Bank ordered the two banks closed.

Eventually, the bank building housed apartments and in 1961 the business of Diercks's Antiques. In 1967 it housed Berlin's Honda Shop.

St. John's Lutheran Church

Frontenac Station

Rev. Johann Christian Friedrich Heyer 1863-1866

Johann Christian Friedrich "Fritz" Heyer, the son of Johan Heyer, master furrier, was born in Braunschweig, Germany. As a young man, he and his wife came to America, where she taught him English. In 1862 he was installed as Pastor of St. John's Evangelical Lutheran Church in Red Wing.

In 1863 Pastor Heyer began gathering the few German-speaking Lutherans living in the Frontenac area, and preached services in the Frontenac School, where women's heads had to be covered in some manner and hymn books consisted of only words, no music, and were printed in German. Women and girls always sat on the north side of the church and the men and boys, on the south side. This custom continued until the early 1920s in German Lutheran churches in Red Wing, Frontenac, Hay Creek, and Goodhue.

Reverend Johann Christian Friedrich "Fritz" Heyer

For three years the few members gathered to hear the Gospel preached to them and by 1866 their numbers were slowly increasing. The opportunities for ministers to come to Frontenac were not very frequent. Pastor Heyer served in the Lutheran Church for a total of fifty-six years.

Pastor C. H. Blecken 1864-1866

Pastor C. H. Blecken, of Hastings, Minnesota, but originally from Hamburg, Germany, was installed as the next pastor of St. John's Lutheran Church in Red Wing, on July 21, 1863.

In 1864 Pastor Blecken conducted monthly services at the schoolhouse in Old Frontenac until 1866.

In 1866 Pastor Blecken formally organized a sister congregation at Frontenac Station, with only twelve members, of which some were listed: J. C. Bennewitz, John Thompson, William Miller, Jacob Schneider, John Roper, John Luth, John Hennings, and Fred Koehn. Bennewitz was the first president of the church, and superintendent of Sabbath School, positions that he held until 1875. That same year (1866) Pastor Blecken resigned, due to an issue over church policies.

Pastor L. Schmidt 1867

In 1867 Pastor L. Schmidt, of Menominee, Wisconsin, was installed as minister at the churches in Red Wing and Frontenac Station, both named St. John's Church, but that same year, it became necessary to call another pastor.

(Goodhue County Historical News)

St. John's Evangelical Lutheran Church 1872

Rev. Christian Bender 1867-1901

Christian Bender was born in the town of Eschelbach, Germany, in 1838, and was the youngest member of a family of sixteen. In 1867 he was sent to this country by the Pilzer Mission Institute of Basil, Switzerland, to serve the German-speaking people, who had immigrated here, which included Red Wing, Frontenac, and other places.

He preached his first sermon at St. John's Lutheran Church in Red Wing on December 7, 1867, with a congregation of thirty-five people.

By 1872, when Rev. Bender was pastor at St. John's Lutheran Church in Red Wing, the congregation at Frontenac had outgrown the schoolhouse, and decided to erect a church, (which was also called St. John's Lutheran Church). A white frame church building 36 by 50 feet, was built at the

Reverend Christian Bender
(Photo courtesy of Barbara Hanson)

An 1887 portrait of the Christian Bender family: Front row, left to right: Mrs. Christian (Christine) Bender, Adolph, Pastor Bender, and Frieda. Back row, left to right: Christine, Anna, Christian Jr., Lydia.

cost of $2,000. J. C. Bennewitz, Jacob Schneider, and William Miller were the building committee, with Gen. Garrard donating the furnace for the church. In 1898 the steeple was added.

The German language was used every other Sunday until 1949; after that, only English was used.

On January 21, 1881, Pastor Bender organized the congregation at West Florence and later that same year, they purchased the Presbyterian Church building for $400, and adopted the name Immanuel Evangelical Lutheran Church. Pastor Bender continued to serve that congregation until 1890.

For nearly thirty-five years, Rev. Christian Bender was the leading German pastor of Goodhue County, until his death in February, 1901.

(Photos and information from the Goodhue County Historical News)

Rev. J. R. Baumann 1901-1914

The same year that Rev. Bender died, the congregation at Frontenac Station was soon given another pastor, Rev. J. R. Baumann. Soon after Rev. Baumann began his new work, he realized that it was necessary for him to begin work in the English language, as the younger generation was rapidly losing the ability to understand the German sermons. Even the smallest children had no benefit from Sunday School because they could not learn the German lessons. From this, it was evident that the congregation could not exist and prosper if English services were not offered to the English-speaking people. Having English

Reverend J. R. Baumann

services attracted many to attend the services, many who would not have benefited from the regular German services.

During his ministry, the congregation grew to some forty families. In 1903 Mrs. Baumann helped to organize the Ladies Aid Society, which purchased a new pulpit, altar, pews, baptismal font, and new organ, which are in use at the time of this writing.

In 1914 Rev. Baumann decided to resign his work at Frontenac Station. His duties in Red Wing were becoming too much for him to handle, and so the congregation accepted his resignation.

Rev. John Baumann, of Red Wing, preached at St. John's Church, in Frontenac, three times a month, for thirteen years, and will deliver his farewell to the members of the congregation, at the installation of Rev. Schaller.

(1914 Daily Republican)

Rev. Winfred Schaller 1914-1919

It was the same year that the congregation decided to have their own pastor. On August 14, 1914, Pastor W. Schaller was installed as the new pastor of St. John's Lutheran Church at Frontenac Station. He was the first resident pastor at the Frontenac church since its organization some forty years earlier. Rev. Baumann, of Red Wing, was in charge of the service, and at noon, the Ladies Aid served dinner at the Florence Town Hall.

Reverend Winfred Schaller

The congregation dedicated its parsonage (cost $3,500) on November 5, 1916. It marked their 50th anniversary. (Photo courtesy of Ken Hoffman)

Ladies Aid Society of St. John's Lutheran Church, organized by Mrs. J. R. Bauman in 1903. (Photo courtesy of Ken Hoffman)

Rev. David Metzger 1919-1922

On November 2, 1919, Pastor David Metzger was installed, and served at St. John's Church until 1922.

Reverend David Metzger

Rev. William Petzke 1922-1928

The church was raised and a basement was added in 1927. In 1928 St. John's of Frontenac and Immanuel of West Florence became a joint parish, served by one pastor. Pastor Petzke had served in Cedar Mills, Minnesota, before taking charge of the newly-formed dual parish.

Reverend William Petzke and family. (Photo courtesy of Ken Hoffman)

Rev. Karl A. Nolting 1928-1949

On November 4, 1928, Karl A. Nolting was installed as pastor of St. John's and Immanuel churches, and served in this position for twenty-one years.

By 1941 the membership had grown to 244. That same year, Pastor Nolting accepted a call to Spring Valley, Wisconsin.

Front row: Rev. Karl and Lucy (Plage) Nolting. Back, left to right: Albert, Paul, and Carl Jr. (Photo courtesy of Ken Hoffman)

On the 80th anniversary in 1946, the stained glass windows (cost $1,417) were dedicated. (Photo courtesy of Barbara Hanson)

Rev. and Mrs. Voigt and sons: Donald, Adelbert, Gerhardt, and Waldemar. (Photo courtesy of Barbara Hanson)

Rev. Walter G. Voigt 1949-1955

Pastor Voigt served the parish starting in 1949, until accepting a call to Merrill, Wisconsin, in 1955.

Rev. Harold Schwertfeger 1955-1962

Reverend Harold Schwertfeger

Rev. Cyrill L. Serwe 1962-1966

Reverend Cyrill Serwe

St. John's Lutheran Church

Roger Woller, Vicar 1967

After completing his second year at the WELS Seminary, Roger Woller was installed as a vicar to serve the congregation for one year.

Rev. Paul Otto 1968-2005

Paul Otto, was installed as Pastor of St. John's Church on July 21, 1968. After thirty-seven years, he retired in 2005.

(Information on the history of St. John's Lutheran Church from the Goodhue County Historical News and "On Eagles' Wings," an illustrated historical review of 125 years of history 1866-1991, at St. John's Church, Frontenac, Minnesota)

Reverend Paul Otto

Church addition 1977

St. John's Evangelical Lutheran Church of Frontenac broke ground for an addition to the church following Sunday worship services. From left to right are: Gary Fitschen, building committee; Norman Gerken, Louis Cushing, and Alvin Baer, all of the church council; Pastor Paul Otto; Virgil Grote, building committee; Ernest Walters, chairman; Wilbur Rieck, Dean Diercks, Harold Grimm, and Donald Steffenhagen, church council. (1977 Daily Republican Eagle)

Creameries

The Jersey Butter and Cheese Factory 1892-1897

Northwest corner of Germania and Brittania streets

(lot 14 in block 2, presently Donna Steffenhagen's corner lot)

In 1892 General Garrard donated land for a new creamery and cheese factory at Frontenac Station. The factory was built by Davis and Rankin, under the supervision of C. H. Freeman of Minneapolis. The building and furnishings cost about $5,600. The wood-frame building was located on the corner of Germania and Brittania streets. The farmers around Frontenac were happy to hear the news of the new creamery, as they had desired a manufactory of this kind, for some time.

A creamery association was organized and the committee in charge of the building operations were M. Ackerman, Theo Freeman, O. D. Reed, Fred Kohn [Koehn?] and Irving Sandt.

The factory stockholders completed the organization as a co-operative association.

The first officers were: President, Charles Luth; treasurer, E. Ackerman; directors, T. E. Freeman, John Gallinger, Irwin Sandt, Charles Sandberg, F. A. Coons, Emma J. Gove, and Miss Mary Westervelt. E. S. Maffit, a graduate of the State Dairy School, was manager.

The factory was a one story frame building, divided into four rooms: the manufacturing room, cheese curing room, office and water cold-storage, with an additional room for the engine and coal, and a covered driveway.

The equipment was one 10 horse engine with 12 horse boiler, horizontal, complete; one centrifugal cream separator known as the jumbo separator, capable of separating 2,500 to 3,000 pounds of milk per hour, one 300 gallon farlamb twin cream vat, one 600 gallon receiving vat and self-agitating attachment; one 400 gallon ash churn, improved, covered with tight and loose pulley, one covered crank suction and force pump; one 300 pound temper tank, piped for steam and water; one farlamb power butter worker, center drip, with tight and loose pulley; one combined power and revolving cheese and curd sink; one single gang cheese press with fourteen cheese hoops; one 600 milk receiver and weighing can; one 600 pound five-beam platform scales; one 400 pound platform milk scales with wheels; steam washing and cleaning tank; one large water tank for supplying boiler, racks and shelves in curing room for curing cheese, also coils of steam pipe on three sides of cheese curing room affording regular temperature, also waster and steam pipes connected with boiler and force pump and to extend through the building to water cold storage vats, butter worker, churn, water tanks for successful operation of the butter and cheese factory.

There were over five hundred people at the grand opening and it was considered one of the largest gatherings in this part of the county. During the forenoon, the creamery was inspected. At noon, dinner was served at the Frontenac Park, and later, speeches were made by W. F. Cross, R. H. Moore, A. F. Anderson and others. In the evening, a grand dance was given in the creamery.

(1892 Daily Republican & Goodhue County Republican)

Creameries

In 1895 F. C. Field leased the creamery for two years.

The stockholders of the creamery held a meeting and decided to sell the creamery to the highest bidder the 1st Monday in April. (1897 Graphic Sentinel)

The Jersey Butter and Cheese factory burned on July 9, 1897, with a total loss of $2,000. The fire originated from the smokestack.

Creamery News
Jersey Butter and Cheese Factory

The milk of a sufficient number of cows to make a certainty the operation of the new Frontenac creamery to its full capacity from the start, has already been subscribed. The creamery will be running in about thirty days.

The Frontenac creamery received 4,680 pounds of milk on Monday and Tuesday 3,300 pounds. After this week, it will require 4,000 pounds daily to supply the factory running at its full capacity.

The Frontenac creamery was closed because the milk sold to the creamery was not sufficient in quantity to make the operation of the plant, pay. The milk of 400 cows would have made the operation of the plant a profitable business, but of late, there has been received hardly one-tenth of that.

The creamery has Lou Schmidt on the road, buying up cream. They also get cream from Lake City, and the prospects are good for next season, with their able manager, James Goff.

The Frontenac creamery lost $800 during the time it was in operation.

(1894 Advance Sun)

Creameries

(Photo of former creamery and now a residence, was allowed by permission of owner)

The Frontenac Co-operative Creamery 1917-1941

In 1917 John Peterson sold a parcel of his land, 50 by 110 feet, for the new Frontenac Co-operative Creamery at Frontenac Station.

The creamery was incorporated in 1917, at a cost of $10,000, of which $4,325 was issued in stock to eighty-seven stockholders. The creamery had twenty-seven more patrons who were not stockholders, in and about Frontenac. The officers of the new organization were Harry Lewis, president; Fred J. Peterson, vice president; R. J. Peterson, secretary and manager; and A. R. Santelman, treasurer. Emmanuel S. Hanson, experienced creamery man and butter maker, was in charge of the creamery.

The company had a modern creamery building with modern equipment and electric power, furnished by the Northern States Power Company. The creamery closed in 1941.

Clarence Wiebusch bought the creamery building in the 1950s and remodeled it for his residence. He raised the roof of the building one story higher. (There is a noticeable difference from the original stone that was used, compared to the cement blocks that were used for the top story.) Clarence was an electrician and also fixed small appliances.

The Possehl family purchased the remodeled creamery building from Clarence Wiebusch in 1959 and lived there until 1987.

Annual Report--1937

FRONTENAC CO-OPERATIVE CREAMERY ASSOCIATION

Frontenac, Minnesota

Officers

PRESIDENT	JOHN P. DAMMAN, Red Wing
VICE-PRESIDENT	FRED J. PETERSON, Lake City
SECRETARY-TREASURER	A. W. GEISLER, Lake City
DIRECTOR	EARL G. HENNINGS, Red Wing
DIRECTOR	FRED W. LUTJEN, Lake City
DIRECTOR	BEN W. SANTELMAN, Red Wing
DIRECTOR	HENRY PLOTE, Lake City
DIRECTOR	FRED J. WIECH, Red Wing

OPERATING STATEMENT

Operator's salary	$999.85
Secretary-treasurer's salary	300.00
Helper-trucker salary	182.37
Directors' fees	92.50
Fuel	332.29
Power and light	187.45
Packing supplies	576.34
Salt	42.21
Acids, butter color, testing supplies	69.43
General supplies	67.46
Office supplies	43.10
Telephone	40.85
Washing powder	38.00
Bank float and service charges	25.35
General expenses	62.70
Freight and drayage	10.50
Repairs	17.80
Insurance	99.29
Taxes	14.94
Interest paid	29.27
Minnesota Unemployment Compensation fund	28.13
Social security fund	15.60
TOTAL OPERATING COST	$3,275.43

GENERAL STATISTICS

Pounds of sweet cream received	288,403
Pounds of 1st grade cream received	26,897
Total pounds of cream received	315,300
Pounds of increase over 1936 receipts	6,373
Average test of cream	28.3
Pounds of butterfat in sweet cream	81,460.3
Pounds of butterfat in first grade cream	7,670
Total pounds of butterfat in cream	89,130.3
Pounds of butter made	110,134
Pounds of overrun	21,008.7
Per cent of overrun	23.56%
Pounds of butter shipped	92,515
Pounds of butter sold to patrons	7,482
Pounds of butter sold locally	10,062
Total pounds of butter sold	110,059
Add closing inventory	378
	110,437
Deduct beginning inventory	303
Total pounds of butter accounted for	110,134
Pounds of increase over 1936 make	3,352
Average price per pound received for butter	32.97c
Average price per pound paid for butterfat	36.72c
Cost to make a pound of butter	2.97c

Creameries

Co-operative Creamery News

The first year of operation, the creamery won an award for their hand separated butter, at the Chicago Dairy Exposition. In 1920 Earl A. F. Paulson, with fifteen years' experience and coming from a family of butter makers, was honored when he won first prize at the Minnesota State Dairymen's convention at Fergus Falls January 18, 19 and 20. Mr. Paulson's butter received a score of 96, and as a special prize, he received a chest of fine community silverware.

(1920 Graphic-Republican)

In 1920 the annual creamery meeting was held at the town hall, where the following officers were elected; president, Harry Lewis, treasurer, Ed Ackerman and secretary, Kirk Hindman.

(1920 Lake City Graphic-Republican)

In the 1920s, the farmers would haul cream to town with horse and wagon. In 1920 E. S. Hanson left the creamery at Frontenac Station and moved his family to Kellogg, where he would manage the creamery there. In 1920 the creamery turned out 104,885 pounds of butter, in 1921, 131,930 pounds, in 1922, 150,852 pounds, and in 1923, 160,875 pounds.

In 1924 Roy Paton was a helper at the creamery, and in the 1930s, Carl J. Nyflot was a butter maker. Harold Grimm picked up and hauled cream from the local farmers to the creamery in the 1930s.

In 1932 Adolph Statski was manager of the creamery with Leonard Schumacher as an employee in 1934.

The Frontenac Co-operative Creamery had its dinner and meeting at the Frontenac Town Hall. The annual report showed the amount of butter made for the year was 106,872 pounds, an increase of 14,699 pounds over the previous year. All officers and directors were re-elected without opposition. Officers were: John P. Damman, president; Fred Peterson, vice president; A. W. Geisler, secretary-treasurer; and five directors, Earl Hennings, Fred Lutjen, Ben Santelman, Fred Wiech, and Henry Plote.

A roast beef dinner was served by the ladies and music was furnished by Caroline Wiech and George Kuhfuss. (1936)

Marshall Laidlaw remembered taking his grandfather's hand (Ed Ackerman) and walking over to the creamery to get a pail of cottage cheese for twenty-five cents.

(A fond memory Marshall Laidlaw told Virginia Oliver)

The Frontenac Co-operative Creamery closed in 1941. Olin O'Daniels, of Lake City, purchased the creamery and removed the machinery and equipment, which he took to Iowa, where he planned on opening a creamery.

Early photo of the Florence Town Hall, with Joe Peters's house on the left. (Photo from the Savage collection)

Florence Town Hall 1875

The township of Florence voted at the late election to build a town hall, to be erected near the Frontenac depot. Mr. Wrigley, of the building committee, informs us that Gen. Garrard will donate the ground for that purpose, and that the hall will be built during the year. Our mechanics will be notified of proposals in due time to put in their bids for the job.

(1874 Wabasha Sentinel)

On April 10, 1875, Israel Garrard deeded lot 8 in block 10 to the township of Florence for one dollar, for a town hall. The building was 34 by 46 feet, with the foundation of limestone, brought from the Frontenac quarry. By 1916 twenty-two more feet had been added to the main room, and that same year, an indoor toilet was added. A kitchen was also added, sometime later.

As the town hall was sitting only a few feet away from the lot line, by 1920, the township purchased lot 9 in block 10 from George Wood Garrard and Virginia H. Garrard, for $150, to be used as a parking lot.

For many years, the town hall was used for board meetings, voting, 4-H meetings, card parties, dances, theatrical plays, township and all general elections, and community gatherings.

In 1990 the Florence Town Hall was updated, with ceilings repaired, fans added, windows restored, and, in 1995, a modern restroom added. In 1994 the Friends of the Florence Town Hall was organized

In 2008 a 12 by 16-foot addition, in the rear of the Florence Town Hall, once used as a kitchen, was converted into a history center for Florence Township.

Original chairs bought at Ferrin's, a furniture store in Red Wing, for $1.25 a piece, are still being used today at town hall meetings and events.

The town hall had a maple floor, which was perfect for dancing, and Bertha Neiderhouser recalls Mr. and Mrs. Albert Keye coming to the dances, wearing wooden Dutch shoes, and dancing in them all night.

Often, there was dancing after the plays, with local musicians providing the music. In 1919 Ervin (Irvin) Terwilliger, a Florence Township farmer, conducted a family orchestra and played throughout the area and Red Wing. One of the Terwilliger boys played the violin, Carrie Luth played the piano, and often, there were several musicians.

Margaret (Fladwed) Hutcheson, of Red Wing, remembered appearing at the town hall in the late 1920s, accompanying her brother, baritone Merritt Fladwed, on the piano. The duo entertained throughout the area and at meetings of the Farm Bureau, which sometimes met at the town hall.

Masquerade balls were held at the town hall in the winter. Corneil Peterson recalled her parents allowing her to briefly see the participants in their costumes, as masquerade balls were considered for adults only at that time.

DANCE!

Frontenac Town Hall

Saturday Evening, July 14

Terwilliger Orchestra Music

Tickets 75c.   Dancing 8 to 12

Florence Town Hall & Town Hall Events

(Photo courtesy of Florence Township History Center)

Unique Curtain

This unique curtain, depicting twenty-five ads of various businesses in Red Wing and Lake City, hangs front stage at the Florence Town Hall. It is unknown who designed and created this colorful curtain, but curtains of this type were found in halls and opera houses throughout the country, during the 1930s and 1940s, and were precursors to television commercials.

This curtain hung on the stage until the town hall interior restoration project in 2003. At that time, it was taken to the Goodhue County Historical Society in Red Wing for cleaning and display. Eventually, township citizens requested it be returned to its home. Black velvet draw curtains can still be used. A colorful curtain at the back of the stage was painted by Celestine Schaller in 1918 for use as a backdrop scene and was rescued from the elements in 1993 when the Friends of the Florence Town Hall inventoried furnishings.

Originally, the town hall did not have a stage. Celestine Schaller, who managed the Frontenac Inn in Old Frontenac for thirty-two years, played an important part in getting an elevated stage and also an addition to the back of the town hall, which was used as a kitchen and is now being used for the Florence Township History Center.

The Play "A Poor Married Man" 1921

The Florence Town Hall had a history of hosting live theater. There was never a shortage of appreciative audiences to enjoy the efforts of the Frontenac Dramatic Club in the 1920s, coached by Celestine Schaller of the Frontenac Inn; in the 1930s groups of friends who enjoyed acting in plays and, about the same time, the Young People's Society of St. John's Lutheran Church were performing "The Wild Oats Boys" at the Town Hall. 4-H clubs also performed plays and skits on stage.

In 1918 the Frontenac Dramatic Club presented "Charley's Aunt," in Belvidere and raised $140 for the Red Cross.

In the 1920s, Corneil Peterson was remembered her part as "Clompie" the Swedish girl. George Akeson often played lead roles. George Possehl, Ethel and Laura Strupe, and Fanny Paton were also some of the regulars.

In the 1930s, Evelyn (Fitschen) Baer played "Polly" the maid in the play "Aunt Samanthy Rules the Roost: a Farce in Three Acts." The play was presented in Frontenac, Belvidere, Oak Center, Hay Creek, Goodhue, and Bellechester. Josephine and Albert Keye [pronounced Ki] were also involved in the acting, production and transportation.

("Friends Remember" from the Friends of the Florence Town Hall newsletter)

Various advertisements of plays put on at the Florence Town Hall

Florence Town Hall Events

The Frontenac String Band will give a social hop at the town hall, Frontenac. The prompter will be O. P. Francisco and the floor managers are Wm. G. Herlinger, L. H. Savage and F. J. Schloer. The tickets will be 75 cents, supper extra. There will be good music and a good time is guaranteed.

(1883)

The dramatic club are working hard in their new and highly interesting play "Everybodys Friend." This is going to be their master effort, and though only amateurs, they certainly have shown themselves superior to any traveling troupe we have seen around here. The attendance at the hall on December 31, 1884, is going to be very large as the coming play is very interesting and a grand dance winds up the entertainment. Tickets can be procured at the post office.

(1884 Lake City Leader)

An entertainment, consisting of vocal and instrumental music, recitations, declamations, question drawer, etc., will be given at the Frontenac town hall, on Friday evening, March 4, 1887, with social and instrumental music by the Frontenac Glee Club, under the management of Mrs. Wm. Herlinger.

(1887 Advance Sun)

Preparations are being made at Frontenac Station for a Grand Bowery Dance, Saturday evening, May 28, to commence at 8 o'clock. The music will be furnished by the Lake City Germania Band and the Frontenac Cornet Band. Jake Glasner will act as prompter and the Frontenac Band as managers. Ed Ackerman and B. W. Dodge, floor managers. The dance will be held in the park. Everybody invited. Tickets 75 cents.

(1887 Graphic)

An entertainment will be given at the Frontenac town hall on January 17, 1890, to obtain funds to purchase a Webster's unabridged dictionary for the Frontenac school district. Admission 10 cents.

(1890 Lake City Republican)

The dance given at the Frontenac town hall, Friday evening, was the greatest social event in that village for a number of years. The attendance was very large, and was composed principally of people from Red Wing and Lake City. Dancing continued until the wee hours, and all participants enjoyed themselves immensely. The music rendered by members of the Mandolin club was excellent, and the dancers, in that vicinity, say they are anxious for a return engagement at an early date.

(1894 Advance Sun)

A grand Thanksgiving celebration will be given at Frontenac on Thursday November 29, 1894. The program includes a big turkey shoot at 10 o'clock in the morning and a grand ball at the town hall in the evening. Music will be furnished by the Frontenac String Band. Floor managers, John Dammann, L. Carlson. L. Schenach, George Mallan, prompter. Tickets will be 75 cents per couple, supper extra at Albert Schmidt's.

(1894 Advance Sun)

The entertainment given by School District No. 26, at Frontenac Saturday evening, was a great success, the hall being packed. All parts were very well rendered, especially the song by Rosa Cook and E. P. Terwilliger's violin solo. The proceeds were over $28, which will go to the library fund.

(1894 Advance Sun)

A social hop will be given at the Frontenac town hall on Friday evening September 21, 1894, with music by the Frontenac String Band, I. D. Hennings prompter, George Johnson is general manager and Ed Schmidt and Lou Carlson floor managers.

(1894 Advance Sun)

The second of the series of masquerade balls at the town hall at Frontenac will be given on the evening of January 26, 1894. The music will be given by the Frontenac String Band, with B. J. Croke as prompter. George Hahn is the manager and Charles Scherf, A. H. Munger and I. Henning are the floor managers.

(1894 Advance Sun)

Next Thursday evening, Thanksgiving Day, there is to be given at the town hall in Frontenac, a ball, with music by the Frontenac String Band. During the day, commencing at 10 a.m., there is to be a turkey shooting match. The tickets for the dance will be $1.00. Supper is to be served at I. G. Munger's.

(1892)

Preparations are being made for an Easter Monday ball to be given at the Frontenac town hall. The music will be by the Frontenac String band with Wm. Bate as prompter. The arrangement committee consists of: A. C. Carolen and W. A. Bate, and the floor managers will be Louis Carlson and P. J. Tomfohr.

(1892)

A grand harvest dance will be held in the town hall at Frontenac, on Friday evening, September 2, 1892. Music will be furnished by the Roberts Bros. full string band. I. D. Hennings will act as prompter. The general managers are H. C. Roberts and O. J. Hennings, floor managers are L. Schenach and W. Bates.

(1892)

The Fourth of July will be celebrated at Frontenac and the eagle will be made to scream on a patriotic manner. There will be a parade headed by the brass band, a game of baseball (Fats vs. Leans), hundred yard foot race, three legged race, wheelbarrow race, horse racing, Derby race, slow race, throwing heavy hammer, high jumping, tug of war, and other games and races. A bowery dance will be given on the new platform, afternoon and evening. If the weather is unfavorable, the dance will be given in the town hall. The arrangement committee consists of Ed Schmidt, H. Heath, Louis Schenach and Fred Meyer."

(1894 Advance Sun)

Frontenac Masquerade; One of the big mask ball successes of the community was that given at Frontenac at which Persell's orchestra of Red Wing furnished the music. The attendance was large and many new, dazzling and bewildering costumes were in evidence. Prizes were awarded as follows; Ladies best, Katherine Morris, Frontenac, gents best, Edward Akerson, best group of three, Maurice Nelson Red Wing, Nora Nelson, Wells Creek, and Rose Martin, Wells Creek, ladies comic, Maggie Peters, Red Wing, gents comic, Albert Keye, Wells Creek, homeliest gents costume, Myron Kells, Wacouta.

(1914)

My Memories Of The Town Hall

Lyle F. Santelman

Lyle F. Santelman, born in 1924, was the son of Elmer and Clara Santelman. In 1921 Elmer and Clara moved to the farmstead just across the road from the school, partway between the two villages, Frontenac Station and Old Frontenac. The farm was owned by August Santelman, Elmer's uncle. August, owned and operated the general store on US Highway 61 at Frontenac Station. In 1945 Elmer and Clara Santelman moved to Red Wing and Lyle entered the Air Force.

Some of my first memories of the Town Hall were the annual Christmas programs that were put on by the teachers and students of the rural school, located between the "Station" and Old Frontenac. Each of the students in the lower grades had a little poem to recite. The older students were involved in the Christmas play or pageant and also all kinds of Christmas carols. It was the kind of program that would not pass politically correct tests today as it was very Christian-oriented. The Christmas program was the highlight of the school year, attended by all the parents and most of the town people.

Some of the other memories of the Town Hall were of the dances that were sponsored by the Florence Township Farm Bureau. The live music was usually supplied by the Kuhfuss Bros. family band. There was usually three or more members of the band. One played the accordion, another a violin and harmonica, a horn player, and also a marimba or xylophone. Occasionally a boy of ten or twelve, son of one of the Kuhfuss brothers, would come and sing some of the songs. He had a beautiful boy soprano voice. After the dance, there was a lunch. Sometimes the women each brought a basket to be sold and at other times, the lunch was provided by a committee of the Farm Bureau.

Some of the other events held at the Town Hall were the annual township meetings. These meetings were held during the winter months and during daylight hours so as not to interfere with the daily chores, so much a part of family farm or field work of spring, summer, and fall.

(Friends of the Florence Town Hall Newsletter)

33923 Highway 61 Blvd. Frontenac, Minnesota 55026

The Florence Town Hall
Erected in 1875

As of 2000, the Florence Town Hall is on the National Register of Historic Places and, today, is the oldest township town hall still in use in the State of Minnesota.

Friends of the Florence Town Hall

...is an organization dedicated to the preservation and continued use of the Florence Town Hall as the township government center, as it has represented self-government, local government and continuity of government in Florence Township since 1875.

Schneider's Groceries and Provisions store on Sclavonia Street, with livery/hotel near the grocery store. (Submitted by Mary Denzer, Lake City from records of Julia Resch)

General Merchandise, Dry Goods, and Grocery Stores

Schneider's Groceries and Provisions 1872-1885
(Jacob Schneider)

After operating a store/tavern/post office, with sleeping quarters on the second floor, in Old Frontenac, Jacob Schneider moved to Frontenac Station around 1872. That same year, Schneider bought land from Israel Garrard (lots 1 and 2 in block 12), and erected a general merchandise, grocery and provisions store on Sclavonia Street, where he dealt in groceries, boots, shoes, wines, and liquor, etc. Schneider's son, William, worked in his father's store until 1878, when he opened his own grocery store, at Frontenac Station (actual location unknown).

A notice in the 1873 Lake City Sentinel stated that Jacob Schneider moved his barn from the village (Old Frontenac) on the river, to the rear of his store at Frontenac Station, for the convenience of farmers who came there to do business.

Jacob Schneider has an elegant pool table and has made many changes for the better in fitting up and painting his store.

(1884 Lake City Leader)

E. J. Megroth, assignee for Jacob Schneider, of Frontenac, informs us that the assets are $2,900 and the liabilities are $5,700.

(1885 Lake City Sentinel)

General Merchandise, Dry Goods, and Grocery Stores

On March 18, 1887, Schneider's wife, Dorothea, died and was buried at Frontenac. The same year, on December 22, 1887, Jacob Schneider married his second wife, Barbara, in Frontenac. By 1892 Jacob and Barbara sold lots 1 and 2 in block 12, to E. A. Kempe. By this time, Jacob Schneider had died and Kempe eventually lost the property. It returned to the widow Barbara Schneider. (An indentation in the hillside, behind the present Adler house, could possibly have been the earlier site of the Schneider store or livery.)

Grocery and provisions store, possibly on Sclavonia Street.

Haustein's Groceries & Provisions 1893
(Casper Frances Joseph Haustein)

Casper Haustein was born in Wacouta on May 9, 1871. His first marriage was to Margaret Catherine Hamm in April 1893. His second marriage was to Anna Sybilla Hamm.

In April 1893, C. F. J. Haustein, also known as "Cap," moved from Red Wing to Frontenac Station and leased a general store on Sclavonia Street. Charles Scherf was an employee at Haustein's store. This building could have been Jacob Schneider's grocery and provisions store after being remodeled and leased to Haustein by E. A. Kempe, then the property owner.

Originally, Casper Haustein ran the Cheap Cash Grocery on the southwest corner of Fifth and Plum streets in Red Wing from 1890 to 1891. After selling his store to Henry Maetzold, Haustein had a grocery store on the corner of Plum and Seventh streets from 1891 to 1892. In 1892 he opened a grocery in H. C. Kohn's wood-frame grocery building, but in 1893 he moved to Frontenac Station, where he opened a grocery and provisions store. Within a year, Haustein partnered with Albert Schmidt at the same site. Returning to Red Wing in 1894, Haustein opened the Spot Cash Grocery on the northeast corner of Bush and

Fifth streets from 1895 to 1896. In 1896 Haustein partnered with Albert Schmidt again at Bush and Fifth streets until 1898 when they dissolved their partnership. Haustein then went into farming until 1929 when he opened a general store at Trout Brook, across from the tannery. C. F. J. Haustein died October 6, 1953

Haustein & Schmidt Groceries and Provisions 1893-1894
(C. F. J. Haustein and Albert Schmidt)

In August 1893, C. F. J. (Casper) Haustein, who already had been conducting a grocery business at Frontenac Station, and Albert Schmidt of Wells Creek formed a partnership, in the new firm of Haustein & Schmidt.

Haustein & Schmidt had a notice in the newspaper in 1894, "We are changing our credit procedure to a strictly cash business and on and after July 1, 1894, no more credit will be given." Another news article stated "Hard times are beginning to show in Frontenac when a man fills his pockets with eggs and sausage at Haustein & Schmidt's."

(1894 Advance Sun)

General Merchandise, Dry Goods, and Grocery Stores

M. Webster & Co. 1866-1871

Since the Goodhue County Abstract files for Frontenac Station do not start until 1872, it is unknown who actually built the building or if this was the exact location of this store, but I feel the store was located on Columbia Street at The Frontenac Cash Store site.

M. Webster & Co. removed their stock of goods from their Lake city store and moved to Frontenac Station where they opened a general merchandise store.

(An ad in the 1866 Lake City Leader)

Murray Bros. Mercantile 1871-1873
(Erastus H. & Dr. R. N. Murray)

Again, the exact location of this store is unknown, but I feel it is possible that Murray Bros. Mercantile store was the successor to Webster & Co., followed in 1873 by the Frontenac Cash Store.

The Murray Bros. have opened out in the mercantile line in Frontenac. We understand they have purchased a general stock of dry goods, groceries, and a variety of such goods as are required by the people of the surrounding country. Frontenac is a progressing town, and the Murray Bros. are the right kind of business men.

(1871 Lake City Sentinel)

This is possibly the building earlier used by M. Webster & Co. and Murray Bros. as their general merchandise store.

General Merchandise, Dry Goods, and Grocery Stores

The Frontenac Cash Store 1873-1874
(H. [Henry] Lorentzen & George H. Dodge)

In October of 1873, H. Lorentzen and George Dodge went into partnership and opened a new store at Frontenac Station, and will keep a full assortment of goods for the country trade. They are reliable men and those who patronize them will be treated honorably. Mr. Lorentzen also has charge of the post office and express office at Frontenac.

(October 1873 Wabasha County Sentinel)

Lorentzen & Dodge, at Frontenac, have fully established themselves in the mercantile business and are ready to wait on customers. Their stock is fresh and their quarters are handy for the farmers who have business to do at the elevator.

(1873 Lake City Sentinel)

George Dodge owned the property next to the Frontenac Cash Store during the time he was in partnership with H. Lorentzen. In 1881 Dodge owned lot 15 in the same block.

The firm of Lorentzen and Dodge, Frontenac, have dissolved. The business will be continued by Mr. Lorentzen. We understand that Mr. Dodge has engaged to the railroad company.

(May 1874 Wabasha County Sentinel)

Later Dodge went into business with Mr. Heslin in a dry goods store at Frontenac Station.

General Merchandise, Dry Goods, and Grocery Stores

The Frontenac Cash Store 1874-1882
(H. (Henry) Lorentzen)

After dissolving partnership with George Dodge in 1874, Lorentzen continued on as proprietor of the Frontenac Cash Store.

Henry Lorentzen was born in Hamburg, Germany, in 1822. By 1857 Henry and Frederica Lorentzen moved to Florence Township. On August 19, 1864, H. Lorentzen was appointed US Postmaster and served until 1893. H. Lorentzen was most likely living in Frontenac Station by 1871, and involved in various businesses.

To the left of The Frontenac Cash Store was the George H. Dodge house (1878), the Peter Swetzer house (1882), and later the residence of August Santelman. (Photo ca. 1912, courtesy of Caroline Earhart)

The Frontenac Cash Store 1882-1885
(H. Lorentzen, Owner)
(Peter Swetzer Sr., Manager)

In 1882 G. H. Dodge & Co. sold their entire stock of goods to Porter (Peter) Swetzer, Esq., who is now beginning to sell goods at a lively rate. He has retained the services of Ben Dodge as bookkeeper and assistant.

(1882 Lake City Review)

"G. H Dodge & Co., Frontenac, have sold their entire stock of goods to Peter Swetzer.

(February 16, 1882, Red Wing Argus)

General Merchandise, Dry Goods, and Grocery Stores

The Frontenac Cash Store 1885-1890
(Frederick & Henry Lorentzen)

Henry and Frederick Lorentzen, were proprietors of the Frontenac Cash Store from 1885 to 1890.

The Frontenac Cash Store 1890-1893
(H. Lorentzen)

In 1890 Frederick Lorentzen relinquished his part of the business to Henry Lorentzen. The Frontenac Cash Store was a general merchandise store, carrying groceries, wines and liquor, notions, and boots and shoes. In 1893 H. Lorentzen relinquished the property back to John Hager.

H. LORENTZEN,
Frontenac, Minn.,
DEALER IN
DRY GOODS,
NOTIONS, BOOTS, SHOES,
Groceries, Hardware,
and in fact everything usually kept in a good store.
Highest Market Price Paid for Wheat.
Farmers Produce, at market price, taken in exchange for all kinds of goods.
Those desiring to purchase any goods in my line will do well to give me a call. Fair dealing is my motto, in all transactions.

A photo of Peter Swetzer in front of The Frontenac Cash Store which he managed in 1882. (Photo ca. 1912, courtesy of Caroline Earhart)

The Frontenac Cash Store 1893-1902
(Lorenz Hoffman)

Lorenz Hoffman came to Red Wing in 1856 and established a steam brewery on Bush Street (which until recently, had been the site of Claydon's Hallmark). He was also associated with the Jacob Christ Brewery in Red Wing. In June 1893, Lorenz Hoffman most likely leased the store from John Hager, and became the proprietor of The Frontenac Cash Store, with John Larson as an employee. Hoffman died in 1912.

General Merchandise, Dry Goods, and Grocery Stores

The Frontenac Cash Store was run by A. R. Santelman and H. L. Hjermstad. (Photo ca. 1912, courtesy of Caroline Earhart)

The Frontenac Cash Store 1902-1916
(A. R. Santelman & H. L. Hjermstad)

The Frontenac Cash Store was established in January of 1902 by August R. Santelman. The store was owned jointly by A. R. Santelman of Frontenac Station and H. L. Hjermstad of Red Wing, with Santelman being the manager.

In 1916 this building was torn down to make way for a newer more modern building on the same site and occupied by the same owners.

August Rudolph Santelman was born in Hay Creek on April 8, 1872, to August Sr. and Maria (Mary) (Meincke) Santelman who were farmers in Hay Creek township. As a young man August was employed at a slaughter house in Red Wing, delivering meat to H. L. Hjermstad's grocery store on Main Street. In 1902, after hearing there was a store for sale at Frontenac Station, H. L. Hjermstad purchased the store and asked August if he would like to go into partnership with him. August agreed and became manager of the store. That same year, on January 30, 1902, August married Mary Steffenhagen. She was born in Frontenac October 1879, the daughter of William and Katherine (Mehrings) Steffenhagen. August and Mary Santelman had three daughters; Ruth, and twins, Helen and Hazel. During their years of growing up in Frontenac, their three daughters helped at the store. They attended school, walking through the marshland when the school was only a one-room school between the two Villages. Eventually, it became a two-room school. In 1909 William Steffenhagen was also working at the store as a clerk.

General Merchandise, Dry Goods, and Grocery Stores

August Santelman purchased a new Maxwell car which came from St. Paul by train. When it arrived at Frontenac Station, August, along with William Steffenhagen went to the train, and with two long pieces of lumber propped onto the flatbed, drove the new Maxwell car off the train. Mary Santelman was one of the first women drivers in that little village.

(Information taken from a video of Ruth, Helen and Hazel being interviewed "What was it like growing up in Frontenac", submitted by Jennifer Stauffer)

By 1915, Hjermstad severed his ties to the mercantile business in Red Wing but kept his grocery business with August Santelman at Frontenac Station, and also his partnership with William Santelman at a grocery store at Claybank.

The Frontenac Cash Store was torn down in 1916 to make way for a more modern grocery on the same site and occupied by the same owners.

Hans Hjermstad was born in Stang, Norway. He came to Red Wing in 1881 and by 1882 entered into the employment of the Boxrud Bros. as bookkeeper at their River Falls, Wisconsin branch store. After one year, he was transferred back to Red Wing and continued on as bookkeeper.

By 1889, brothers, H. L. and C. O. Hjermstad bought the interest in Peter Kempe's grocery. Kempe was occupying one of the Boxrud stores at 415 Main street. The Hjermstad Bros. entered into the grocery business for themselves and were known as the H. L. Hjermstad Co.

Besides his grocery, crockery and glassware store in Red Wing, H. L. Hjermstad went into a partnership with August R. Santelman, jointly owning and operating the Frontenac Cash Store at Frontenac Station, in 1902.

In 1910 the Boxrud Bros. incorporated with H. L. Hjermstad to form the Boxrud & Hjermstad Company in Red Wing.

By 1915, H. L. Hjermstad assumed the position of secretary and manager of the Citizen's Fund Mutual Fire Insurance Co. A few years later, he became the president of the company, a position he held until his death in 1931.

General Merchandise, Dry Goods, and Grocery Stores

On the left was Santelman & Hjermstad's Frontenac Cash Store, built in 1916. To the right of the store was the home of William and Nancy Herlinger from the 1870s to 1905. Nancy Herlinger conducted a boarding house at their residence, starting in 1873.

Santelman and Hjermstad's new grocery store was built in 1916, a stucco building thirty feet by seventy feet. Unfortunately, in 1925 the store was destroyed in a fire, but was soon rebuilt. This is the present building, which stands today and formerly housed Wee Three & Mee.

"William Herlinger, at Frontenac Station, is erecting a large addition to his residence. We learn that they are prepared to accommodate train men and travelers with meals and lodging when called upon. This is a necessity supplied, and should be well patronized."

(1873 Lake City Sentinel)

After William Herlinger's death, in 1903, Mrs. Herlinger sold the house to William Steffenhagen, in 1905, and she moved to Seattle, Washington. John and Frieda Steffenhagen would then become the next owners, in 1910.

The house was later remodeled into a restaurant.

FRONTENAC CASH STORE
A. R. SANTELMAN, Mgr.
QUALITY & SERVICE
Lake City 783   Red Wing 40F12

General Merchandise, Dry Goods, and Grocery Stores

The Frontenac Cash Store built in 1916, and the Steffenhagen Residence.

"Frontenac Cash Store Destroyed By Fire" 1925

In 1925 the Frontenac Cash Store, operated by A. R. Santelman and owned by Mr. Santelman and H. L. Hjermstad, was completely destroyed by fire, which was discovered about 1 o'clock in the morning. It was possibly due to an overheated furnace. An appeal was sent to the Lake City Fire department for aid but before they could arrive, the building had been consumed. The loss on the building and its contents was estimated between $11,000 and $12,000, covered by insurance of 60 percent.

The fire was discovered by John Akeson, living about two blocks from the store, who noticed the flames from a window in his home.

An alarm was sounded and the entire population of Frontenac Station was soon on the scene. The flames had already made such headway that it was impossible to salvage any of the stock or fixtures. Only the bare walls of the store remained.

A bucket brigade was formed to prevent the fire from destroying the neighboring Steffenhagen house. Considerable damage was done, but the house was not destroyed.

(article in the 1925 Lake City Graphic-Republican)

Rebuilding the store was decided on and temporary quarters were secured in William and Grace Wiech's pool hall, next door, where business would be carried on until more permanent quarters could be found.

General Merchandise, Dry Goods, and Grocery Stores

1931 photo of Santelman's store & car. (Photo courtesy of Revoir Collection - GCHS)

Santelman's Grocery Store 1931

After H. L. Hjermstad's death in 1931, August and Mary Santelman took over full ownership of the Frontenac Cash Store and changed the name to Santelman's which they ran from 1931 to 1943.

Inside Santelman's grocery store are August Santelman and his three brothers, Ben, Henry, and George, ca. 1941. (Photo courtesy of GCHS)

August Santelman standing outside his grocery store. (Photo courtesy of Jeni Stauffer)

General Merchandise, Dry Goods, and Grocery Stores

August Santelman waiting on customer, Leonard Akeson, who operated the Shell Oil station across from Santelman's grocery on Highway 61.

August Santelman, his wife Mary, their three children, Ruth, twins Hazel and Helen, and good friend, John Thimijan who lived with August and Mary. ca. 1912 (Photo courtesty of Jeni Stauffer, great granddaughter of August Santelman)

After forty-two years in the grocery business, August and Mary Santelman sold their grocery store on August 1, 1943 to Mr. and Mrs. Sumner A. Rice. The Rices' had recently been the proprietors of the Country Club tavern in Frontenac Station

Lester "Tac" Tackaberry's Ice Cream Shack. Lester Tackaberry standing in front of his ice cream shack with his wife, "Nettie" leaning against a Harley Davidson motorcycle. The ice cream shack was located between the Santelman and Tackaberry properties next to Highway 61.

General Merchandise, Dry Goods, and Grocery Stores

August and Mary Santelman's old house, next to highway 61, getting ready to be moved to another lot. It was also the former home of the Peter Swetzer family, in 1882 (Photo courtesy of Jeni Stauffer)

Barn next to Santelman's old house. (Photo courtesy of Jeni Stauffer)

General Merchandise, Dry Goods, and Grocery Stores

August and Mary Santelman's new home on the former site, on the northwest corner of Highway 61 and Scandinavia Street. (Photo courtesy of Jeni Stauffer)

Santelman's Memorable Moments

A story that Alice Tackaberry recalls was when August Santelman was helping Mrs. Santelman put on storm windows. Mrs. Santelman was on a ladder and turned to reach for a window from August, when he disappeared into the ground. There had been a large amount of rainfall earlier in the day. The board covering the cistern and the ground around the cistern gave way and August fell into the well. Alice Tackaberry had been outside her house, pruning her flowers, when she heard calls for help. She ran over to find August deep down in the well. Alice ran home to get a rope, which they threw down to August but, as Alice was small a woman and August was known to be quite heavy, Alice could not pull him up. Alice noticed people coming out of Santelman's grocery store across the street, and yelled for their help. They finally got August out of his predicament. Alice still has in her garage the rope that was used to help pull August Santelman from his cistern.

General Merchandise, Dry Goods, and Grocery Stores

In 1917 August Santelman was badly burned at his store when a can of wood-alcohol exploded as he started to pour some of the liquid into a lighting plant. He had used a small quantity of alcohol in an effort to heat the generator and was under the impression that it had burned out. The moment he poured additional liquid into the machine, the explosion followed. Santelman was practically enveloped in flames. His clothing was burned off his body to the waist and had it not been for the fact that Mrs. Santelman came to the rescue, he might have suffered fatal injuries.
(1917 Red Wing Daily Republican)

Chicago Boys Rob Frontenac Store

Cutting through a screen door and entering the Frontenac Cash Store, while the owner A. R. Santelman was upstairs at dinner, two fourteen-year-old Chicago youthful runaways, emptied the cash register of $50 and made away before Mr. Santelman became aware of the loss.

Following a search, which lasted until nightfall, the boys were caught on the old territorial road near the T. J. Walters farm, about three miles from Lake City, the money still in their possession. The boys were caught by four men riding with Mr. Santelman, and the boys were taken to Red Wing and locked up. They would probably be turned over to the Chicago authorities when the case comes up before the juvenile court.
(1920 Lake City Graphic-Republican)

In 1924 a burglar broke into Santelman's Frontenac Cash Store by breaking a window in the basement. He fitted himself up with Santelman's sheep lined coat, flannel shirt, sweater, a good pair of trousers, high top boots and a pair of rubbers. He also took a handful of pennies from the cash register. He left his old clothes in the store.
(Graphic-Republican 1924)

Vandals, whose identity has not been determined, wrecked havoc at the Frontenac Cash Store, operated by A. R. Santelman, Monday night. The six-plate glass windows were smashed, causing damage at around $210. Authorities are investigating and expect to round up the guilty parties.
(1933)

General Merchandise, Dry Goods, and Grocery Stores

Rice's Store 1943-1960
(Sumner "Sam" and Mabel Rice)

CLEARANCE SALE
LADIES' SLACKS
50% Wool, 50% Rayon
Sizes 12 to 20.
$4.39
Corduroy sizes 12 to 20.
$5.68
RICE'S STORE
Frontenac, Minn.

Sumner and Mabel Rice purchased August Santelman's grocery store, and took possession on August 1, 1943. Sam was a very meticulous man who believed in having a strict schedule for cleaning and maintaining his store and property.

Eventually Rice's Store became the headquarters for the bus depot. It cost twenty-five cents to ride from Frontenac Station to Red Wing, and thirty-five cents if you lived outside of Frontenac; four Greyhound buses stopped there daily. Sam and Mabel ran the grocery store until 1960, when Victor and Harriet Holter took over the store.

Sumner A. Rice was born August 1, 1893, to Erastus and Amelia (Weiser) Rice, in Ellsworth, Pierce County, Wisconsin. His siblings were Floyd B., Harold D., Walter R. and Eveline M. Rice.

In 1910, at the age of sixteen, Sumner, or Sam, as many people called him, was working as a farm laborer on the Andrew and Emma Fink farm in Wisconsin. By 1930 Sumner and Mabel Irene Rice were living in La Crosse, Wisconsin, where Sam worked as a retail salesman for a furniture store. By 1936 he, Mabel, and his mother-in-law, Mary Luke, had moved to Frontenac Station, where they bought lots 1, 2, 3, and 4 in block 9 on Germania Street, which included Ernest Alpers's former confectionery store. The Rices remodeled the store for their residence.

From 1939 to 1943, Mr. and Mrs. Sumner Rice managed the Country Club tavern, owned by Ed Peters (presently B. Wells). In 1943 Sam and Mabel Rice bought August Santelman's grocery store, which they ran until 1960.

Butch Berlin relates various stories; when he was a young boy, Sam Rice would give Butch fifteen cents to hold the watering hose while Sam very carefully watered his plants and vegetable garden. Sam wanted things done correctly and they had to be done perfectly.

Sam would always measure his grass before cutting, as the grass had to be 2¾ inches high before he would mow.

General Merchandise, Dry Goods, and Grocery Stores

There was always a continuous feud between Sumner Rice and his neighbor, Albert Tomforde, "the Dutchman," who operated the Frontenac Restaurant. The issue was always neatness.

Mabel Rice died December 8, 1969, and Sumner A. Rice died March 17, 1975. Both are buried in Oakwood Cemetery in Red Wing.

Sumner Rice residence on Germania Street, purchased in 1936. (formerly Alpers's Confectionery)

Holter's Sausage and Cheese Shop 1960-1974

(Victor and Harriet Holter)

Holter's Sausage and Cheese Shop 1974-1998

(William S. and Lois Holter)

Bill and Lois Holter were second-generation owners of Holter's Sausage and Cheese Shop, which carried an extensive line of cheeses, sausages, and smoked fish. They also served campers at Frontenac State Park with camping supplies and groceries.

(Staff story and photo by Gary Cox, Eagle Extra, 1983)

William and Lois Holter.

63

Lots 11, 12, and 13, Block 8
(presently The Whistle Stop)

Schneider's Grocery Store 1878-1880

(William Schneider)

Since Goodhue County Abstract files did not start until 1872 for Frontenac Station, it is unknown what year this store was built or who built the building.

Lots 12 and 13 in block 8 were owned by John Sauter from 1873 to 1882, and again from 1888 until 1926, when it was purchased by Ackerman & Gercken.

Although it is not a known fact that this was Schneider's store, an educated guess places him at this location.

In 1872 William Schneider worked in his father's grocery and provisions store on Sclavonia Street on the south side of the village. In 1874 William married Charlotte Fraund, born in Germany in 1854. In the spring of 1878, William Schneider opened his own grocery store at Frontenac Station. Meanwhile, over the years, several people leased or rented the building for their grocery business.

(Photo courtesy of Florence Township History Center)

General Merchandise, Dry Goods, and Grocery Stores

Dodge & Heslin Dry Goods 1880-1882

(George H. Dodge and Heslin)

George Hooper Dodge moved from Mt. Pleasant, Wabasha County, to Frontenac Station in 1873. From 1873 to 1874, George H. Dodge was in partnership with H. Lorentzen at the Frontenac Cash Store, then the partnership was dissolved.

George Dodge purchased lots 12 and 13 in block 8 from John Sauter in 1882 and also owned lots 15 and 16 in block 8 from 1878 to 1882. I suspect Dodge & Heslin used the later White Store building for their dry goods store during this time. George's brother, Benjamin clerked at the store. Dodge & Heslin dissolved their partnership in 1882.

G. H. Dodge & Company 1882

(George H. and Benjamin Dodge)

George Hooper Dodge was born in Maine in 1850, the son of Benjamin W. and Elizabeth Dodge. During the 1860s and 1870s, his family was living in Wabasha County. His brothers were Elbridge and Benwalter, both born in Maine. By 1880, George was married to Harriet Jane Westervelt and living at Frontenac Station. In 1882 Dodge dissolved partnership with Heslin at their dry goods store at Frontenac Station. Soon after, George and his brother Benwalter went into partnership in the firm of G. H. Dodge & Company at the same site. For some unknown reason, the same month the brothers sold their business to Peter Swetzer.

G. H. Dodge & Co. represents the new firm name.
(February 1882 Lake City Review)

"G. H. Dodge & Co., Frontenac, have sold their entire stock of goods to Peter Swetzer."
(February 16, 1882, Red Wing Argus)

George Hooper Dodge moved to Minneapolis, Minnesota, in 1882 where he took up bookkeeping, and later went into real estate. George H. Dodge died in 1924 in Minneapolis, Hennipen County.

Ackerman & Son 1885-1894

(Michael Ackerman and his son, Edward Ackerman)

Mr. Ackerman has rented the store building formerly occupied by Jacob Schneider at Frontenac, and will put in a first class line of goods. He is a good business man.
(1885 Lake City Sentinel)

Perhaps the newspaper meant William Schneider, as Jacob Schneider was still operating his own store on Sclavonia Street.

The store was first established in 1885 by E. M. Ackerman and known as E. M. Ackerman & Son. The building was 22 by 50 feet in size, with a story addition of 22 by 40 feet. It carried a complete line of that of a general store.
(1924 Lake City Graphic-Republican)

In 1894 an ad stated that Ackerman & Son had gone strictly to a cash business and no more credit would be given.

The White Store 1907-1915

(William H. Savage)

William Henry Savage was born June 22, 1864, on his parents' farm in Florence Townhip; he still owned this farm at the time of his death. He was the third son of Marietta and Harvey Savage. He was educated in the local schools and attended Carlton College in Northfield for one year. He graduated from Cornell College in Mount Vernon, Iowa, in 1886, specializing in civil engineering.

He taught in public schools for a few years, and then followed his chosen work, surveying, in the states of Washington, Idaho, and Montana for ten years.

Returning to Frontenac, he farmed for a few years and then in 1907 he leased the former Ackerman & Son Grocery Store. Savage managed the store until 1915, with Joseph Gercken as clerk.

Savage took an active part in the public affairs of the community, and was town treasurer and school board clerk, for a number of years. William Savage died in 1935 and is buried at the Frontenac Cemetery.
(From the genealogy of the Charles Savage family)

General Merchandise, Dry Goods, and Grocery Stores

Edward Ackerman far left, possibly Richard Grimm, clerk, Irma Ackerman, and on the far right Joe Gercken. (Photo courtesy of Florence Township History Center)

The White Store 1915-1932
(Edward Ackerman & Joe Gercken)

Edward Ackerman was in partnership with Joe Gercken at The White Store from 1915 until 1932. The store had an ice cream parlor on the left side, gas pumps in front of the store, and living quarters in the back. In 1924 Richard H. Grimm clerked in the store for Ackerman and Gercken. (As a young boy, Marshall Laidlaw worked in his grandfather Edward Ackerman's store.)

Due to poor health, Ed Ackerman was forced to retire and in 1932 The White Store was sold to partners, Hindman and Wohlers.

The present firm was made in 1915. It carries an investment of $4,500 in a complete line of a general store. Gasoline and lubricating oil are handled by the store. The firm owns their own building, 22 by 50 feet in size, with a story addition of 22 by 40 feet. The store is called the "White Store" because it is painted white, both inside and outside.

(1924 Lake City Graphic-Republican)

General Merchandise, Dry Goods, and Grocery Stores

An advertisement plate given by Ackerman & Gercken in 1920 to their customers, in appreciation of their business at The White Store.

THE WHITE STORE
OF FRONTENAC

General Merchandise

GASOLINE & OIL   ICE CREAM PARLOR

LADIES' REST ROOM

LET US SERVE YOU

Service is Our Motto

ACKERMAN & GERCKEN, Props.

The White Store
ACKERMAN & GERKEN, Props
Frontenac   Minnesota

The Store that Saves You Money

Below are a few of the money saving values in good merchandise that are being offered at this store on

Wednesday   Thursday   Saturday
April 8   April 9   April 11

There are many more bargains not listed waiting for you to call and look them over

PERCALES—Fast colors, yard 16½c. Dress Ginghams, yard 17½c. Happy Home House Frocks, 99c and $1.19, all stlyes, sizes 36 to 52.

HOSE—Mens black cotton socks, lisle finish, pair 10c; Womens black cotton hose, wide top, seamed back, high spliced heel and toe, double sole, pair 19c.

SHIRTS—Chambray work shirts, med. blue at 78c

OVERALLS—Blue Bell 220 Overalls, one of America's best made overalls, triple stitched, pair $1.48

HOUSE BROOMS—good quality corn, wire bound neck, four sewed with extra strong twine, 49c

20 Pounds Granulated Sugar, $1.36
This brings it down to 6 4-5c a lb.

We take Eggs in exchange for merchandise and pay the highest market price

General Merchandise, Dry Goods, and Grocery Stores

A Red Wing Pottery bean pot, advertising Hindman & Wohlers store at Frontenac Station, given to customers in appreciation of their business. Today, this is a highly sought-after collectible.

The White Store 1932-1935

(Kirk E. Hindman and Emil Wohlers)

In 1930 Kirk Emerson Hindman was the cashier at the Frontenac State Bank. The bank closed in 1932, and that same year Hindman became a partner with Emil Wohlers, conducting The White Store.

In 1935 Hindman & Wohlers sold their store to Harold Sundberg of Red Wing, but Wohlers stayed on to manage the store for Sundberg.

After selling the store in 1935, Hindman and his family moved to Red Wing, where he took the job as advertising manager for the Red Wing newspaper. Kirk Emerson Hindman died in Red Wing in April 1959.

A gunny sack shopping bag advertising Hindman & Wohlers, The White Store. (photo courtesy Wayne Miller)

Modern Store at Frontenac Station

The Sundberg Store at Frontenac, formerly the "White Front," which provides for that community the most efficient service as regards purchases of foods.

Sundberg's Food Market 1935-1939
(Harold Sundberg)

Harold Sundberg purchased The White Store from Hindman and Wohlers in 1935 and changed the name to Sundberg's Food Market. Wohlers stayed on and managed Sundberg's grocery store for the next four years.

Harold Sundberg owned three stores in Red Wing, one in Goodhue, and one at Frontenac Station. His main grocery store was on the southeast corner of Main and Plum streets. He also had the Clover Farm Store on Third Street, run by Ken Paulson, the West End Grocery on Old West Main Street, and a grocery store in Goodhue, in the corner of the Anderson building on Broadway. Sundberg had four delivery trucks that traveled more than 100,000 miles during the year, making deliveries to his customers.

In 1939 Wohlers took over ownership of Sundberg's Food Market.

General Merchandise, Dry Goods, and Grocery Stores

The White Store 1939
(Emil Wohlers)

When Emil Wohlers took over Sundberg's Food Market, which he had already been managing for Sundberg for the past four years, he changed the name back to The White Store.

Emil and Emma Wohlers had four children: Robert, Dorothy, Kenneth, and Merlyn.

That same year (1939), Emil Wohlers sold his grocery store to Julius Schmidt and in 1942 Wohlers moved to California, where he died in 1945. He is buried in Frontenac.

The White Store 1939-1946
(Julius F. Schmidt)
(presently The Whistle Stop site)

In 1939 Julius Schmidt purchased The White Store from Emil Wohlers, who had just recently acquired the store from Harold Sundberg.

In 1946 Schmidt retired and, unfortunately, died that same year.

Charlson's White Grocery 1946-1952
(Rudy and Maxine Charlson)

In 1946 Charlson's White Grocery was managed by Rudy and Maxine Charlson. From 1946 to 1947, Mrs. L. Maxine Charlson housed the post office in her grocery store and was acting postmaster for about a year.

In 1952 the Charlsons demolished their grocery building and, in its place, had a new service station erected. That same year, Charlson sold the station to Wally Sr. and Doris Berlin.

ANNOUNCEMENT

I have purchased the grocery business of Emil Wohlers at Frontenac and have already taken possession.

Continuance of your patronage and good will will be appreciated.

WHITE STORE
FRONTENAC, MINN.
JULIUS SCHMIDT, PROP.

A TOAST *to an* **AMERICAN Christmas**

May it be one of continuous joy, made richer by the loyalty of friends and loved ones everywhere. We give you "A Merry American Christmas."

Charlson's White Grocery
Rudie and Maxine Charlson
Frontenac

Leo Sauter's confectionery store, ca. 1921, with Leo Sauter's garage on the far left. (Photo from the Revoir collection, GCHS)

Sauter's Confectionery 1920-1922
(Leo Sauter)
(presently B. Wells)

Leo Sauter built a confectionery store in 1920 on the southern part of lot 7, on block 9, according to Vic Wiech. (According to the Red Wing Directory, Leo Sauter was the proprietor of a confectionery store from 1920 to 1922.) In 1922 Sauter sold his confectionery store to Edward and Louis Peters, who remodeled the building, for the Peters Bros. Bar and Billiard business.

Leo built Sauter's garage in 1921, which was located on the northern part of lot 7 in block 9.

General Merchandise, Dry Goods, and Grocery Stores

Alpers's Confectionery 1927-1934
(Ernest Alpers)

Ernest Alpers was born in Germany on June 9, 1891, and came to America with his parents when he was a year old. By 1920 the family had settled in Florence Township. By 1924 Ernest was bartending at his father's soft drink parlor.

In 1927 Ernest Alpers, a single young man with a jovial nature, purchased lot 4 in block 9 from John Damman and became the proprietor of a confectionery store.

A tragic accident involving a train took Ernest Alpers's life in 1934. The accident happened at the Milwaukee Railroad crossing, just east of the Milwaukee depot. It was thought that Alpers was on his way home, on the south hillside, and was struck by a westbound Milwaukee freight train. A theory of foul play came into play when Alpers was found with no money in his pockets, when each night he always took the day's receipts home. Robbery could have been a motive and someone could have laid Alpers on the tracks to make it look like he was run over by a train. A verdict of accidental death, following a coroner's investigation, was finally given for the death of Ernest Alpers at the age of forty-three.

Ernest Alpers was survived by his two brothers, John Henry and Frank, and five sisters; Katherine Alpers of Frontenac, L. H. Fellman of Wacouta, Mrs. W. R. Paton, Mrs. R. A. Paton, and Miss Florence Alpers, all of Red Wing.

In 1936 Ernest Alpers's Confectionery store, on Germania Street, was purchased by Sumner "Sam" Rice and he remodeled it for his residence.

(Photo courtesy of Butch Berlin)

Restaurants

Berlin's Coffee Shop 1952-1974
(Wally Sr. and Doris Berlin)
(formerly The White Store site)

At the age of two years, following the death of her mother, Doris Berlin went to live with relatives on a farm between Zumbrota and Wanamingo. She could only speak Norwegian, but learned English when she went to country school. She came to Red Wing for her senior year of high school, and upon graduation, went to work at Woolworth's to save money to go to college. She met Wally Berlin when he approached her to ask for her address for his friend, whom she had previously dated. The friend never got her address because Wally was so interested in her that in five months he had given her a ring. They married two years later.

Wallace and Doris Berlin.

Wally and his father, "Tuntz" Berlin, owned the filling station at the foot of the old Red Wing high bridge, plus other stations in the area. When the new bridge was going to be built, they had to give up their property, so he scouted the Frontenac Station area for a new location for his filling station.

In 1952 Rudy and Maxine Charlson demolished their Charlson's White Grocery Store and, at the same site, built a filling station.

Restaurants

Unable to find a home to purchase, the Berlins purchased Charlson's building and cleared away the remnants of the old store still left on the property, and moved into the filling station in October with son, Wally Jr. "Butch," and daughter, Barbara. They made what is now the front dining room of the café into their living room.

The introduction to town became unpleasant in November when two boys from the training school robbed them at gun- and knifepoint, taking their money and car.

Shortly after they settled in, men who were working for the rural electric co-op came around to homes in Frontenac Station looking for a place to buy lunch. Doris was the only one willing to provide it. Wally and his father, Tuntz Berlin, moved a large table into their living room, built a counter with seven stools, and a restaurant was born. Shortly after, Wally and Doris opened it as "Berlin's Coffee Shop." The coffee shop and restaurant seated twenty-six people, with Berlins' residence in the rear of the building. They had Standard gas pumps but, with encouragement from Elmer Bengston, changed to Texaco gas pumps. Eventuall, the restaurant became Berlin's Café.

FISH FRY
Fish Fried to Golden Perfection with full Buffet **$1.25**
Baked Beans, French Fries, potato salad, tuna salad, Glocified rice, cold slaw, relishes, rolls and butter
Children 6 & Under **50¢**
Every Friday 5 p.m. to 9 p.m.
"The Family Restaurant with Family Prices"
BERLIN'S CAFE
In Scenic Frontenac

Berlin's Café

In 1964 Berlin doubled the size of the restaurant by adding a dining room onto the building. Wally and Doris ran Berlin's Café for twenty-two years, with a barber shop, filling station, and café in the same building. Business boomed, especially on Friday nights when they had a fish fry. Customers lined up around the outside of the building. The whole family worked to serve them all. Wally's father would do haircuts, someone else would sell shoes, and they all took turns pumping gas. Sometimes they would serve three hundred people in a restaurant holding less than thirty people at a time.

Students from the Villa Maria would fill the café at times and, when Doris didn't have enough waitresses, would pitch in, taking orders, frying hamburgers and fries, and making the milkshakes. Berlins sold their café in 1974.

(Article from the Friends of the Florence Town Hall Newsletter)

Clarence R. "Tuntz" Berlin

Originally, Berlin's Café had two front entrances. Wally's father, Clarence "Tuntz" Berlin, had his barbershop on the right side of the building, with its own entrance. (Today, the barbershop would have been where the bathrooms are now).

In 1967 Wally Berlin Sr. opened a motorcycle shop, which he and Wally Jr. "Butch," operated until December 1984, when Wally Sr. sold the cycle shop to Greg Coffman.

Shortly after, Wally Sr. and Butch bought the old Fiesta Restaurant building on Highway 61, outside of Red Wing, which had been empty for many years, and opened a used car dealership. Butch Berlin still runs Wacouta Motors at that same site, as of 2014.

Clarence Berlin

Restaurants

The original home of Albert and Bertha (Schenach) Schmidt, in 1908, which was later restored by Bill and Judy Steffenhagen. (1975 photos courtesy of Judy Steffenhagen, Lake City)

Photo taken in 1975 of Ryan and Lane Steffenhagen with neighborhood friends, Steve Marshman, Brian Heins, Mark and Clark Flen, and Jr. (Butch) Berlin. (Photo courtesy of Judy Steffenhagen)

Restaurants

The Whistle Stop 1974-1975
(Linda Farrington & Ron Schummer)

In July 1974 Wally and Doris Berlin sold their cafe to Linda Farrington and partner Ron Schummer. The name of the cafe was changed to The Whistle Stop probably in association with the trains that came through Frontenac Station. The Farrington-Schummer partnership ended after one year.

The Whistle Stop 1975-1985
(Richard & Linda Farrington)

Linda Farrington and her brother Richard operated the Whistle Stop for the next ten years. In 1985 they sold the restaurant to Carolyn Elwood.

The Whistle Stop 1985
(Carolyn Elwood)

The Whistle Stop 1995
(Diane Holahan)

The Whistle Stop 1995-2000
(Darla Potterf)

While operating the restaurant, Darla lived next door in the old Albert Schmidt house.

The Whistle Stop 2000-2004
(Marcia Damman)

The Whistle Stop 2004-current
(Dan and Carol Davidson)

Through the years, there were various owners of the Whistle Stop, including Ed Searles who also owned The Galley, in Lake City.

Restaurants

Traveling through Frontenac Station on US Highway 3, ca. 1930 (Photo courtesy of GCHS)

    The house on the far left was the William Herlinger residence and boarding house during the 1870s, and later, the Frontenac Eat Shop, operated by William and Grace Wiech during the 1920s and 1930s, and the Frontenac Restaurant run by Albert Thomforde from 1940 until 1971, when it burned down.

Grace Wiech in front of the Frontenac Eat Shop in the 1920s, along with Annie Sauter, Don Wiech and his wife, Vonnie (Don is Victor Wiech's brother). (Photo courtesy of Vic Wiech and Marjorie Dunbar)

Frontenac Eat Shop 1928-1935
(William H. and Grace [Lindquist] Wiech)

William Henry Wiech was born in Red Wing in 1896, the son of Johann and Eliza Wiech. In 1910, the Wiech family was living in Hay Creek. The children were: Anna, Amelia, Elize, Kate (Catarina) Julius, Fred and William. William attended Red Wing schools and also the Red Wing Business College. In 1917, William married Grace Lindquist and they had two children Victor and Don Wiech. By 1920, William and Grace were farming and living near Frontenac Station.

In 1928 Grace Wiech purchased property from Nancy Herlinger, where William and Grace Wiech opened the Frontenac Eat Shop, on US Highway 3, at Frontenac Station. Their living quarters were above their business. The restaurant/tavern/pool hall was located next door to the Frontenac Cash Store, which was then being run by Santelman & Hjermstad. Later William and Grace divorced, and Grace continued to run the business.

In 1935 William married Anna Carr. They farmed in the Frontenac area, and later, William worked at Meyer Machine in Red Wing. Earlier, he had operated Wiech's Heating in Hager City, Wisconsin. William Wiech died at Hager City, Wisconsin, on June 21, 1981. (William and Grace were Victor Wiech's parents.)

Restaurants

Grace Wiech, standing behind the counter in her restaurant/bar, in the mid-1930s. (Photo courtesy of Vic Wiech and daughter, Marjorie Dunbar)

Frontenac Eat Shop 1935-1939
(Grace Wiech)

Answering an alarm, the Lake City Fire Department made a run to Frontenac Station, where they found a roof fire at the restaurant and tavern operated by Mrs. Grace Wiech. A hole had been burned in the roof and the blaze was underway with a strong wind to fan it. The wind direction was such that, had the blaze got out of control, several other buildings would have been in danger. Damage was confined to the roof with the exception of the water damage to lower floors.

(1939 Lake City Graphic-Republican)

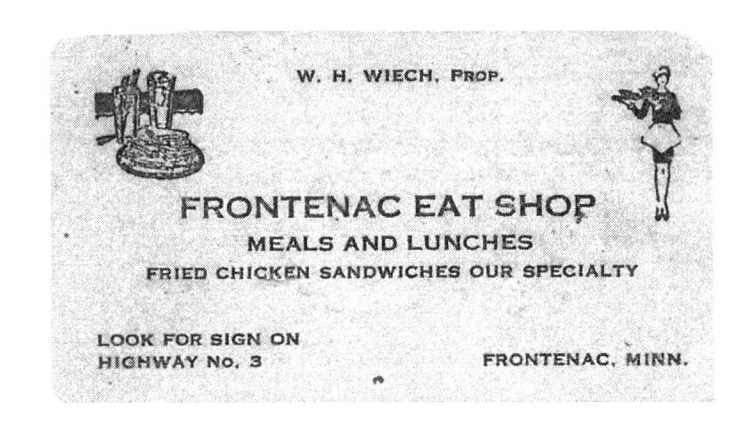

W. H. WIECH, PROP.

FRONTENAC EAT SHOP
MEALS AND LUNCHES
FRIED CHICKEN SANDWICHES OUR SPECIALTY

LOOK FOR SIGN ON
HIGHWAY No. 3   FRONTENAC, MINN.

Restaurants

Frontenac Restaurant 1940-1971
(Albert "the Dutchman" and Grace [Wiech] Tomforde)

Albert Dietrich Tomforde was born in Ahlerstedt, Germany, in 1898, and in 1925, he immigrated to the United States. His first wife was Maria Margaretha Alphers of Mt. Pleasant, Wabasha County. They had one daughter. Maria died at the age of 32, in 1930.

According to Butch Berlin, Albert had fought in the German Army during World War I but after coming to America and becoming a U S citizen, Albert later fought in the U S Army during World War II.

Butch Berlin recalled a favorite memory he had of Albert "the Dutchman" Tomforde. Albert always made his own dandelion wine and on Halloween night when Butch and his older friends went trick and treating with a group of younger children they would stop at Albert's residence and he would give the younger children candy and then Albert would ask the older boys, in his heavy German accent, "vich do you vant", and he would hold out a cigar in one hand and a glass of his homemade wine in the other hand.

Berlin also recalled that Albert was not the best driver and would slowly back out of his garage until he bumped into Sam Rice's garage. Albert and Sam had an on-going feud for many years.

About 1940 Albert Tomforde married Mrs. Grace Wiech, who was operating the "Frontenac Eat Shop". They changed the name of the restaurant/bar/pool hall to the "Frontenac Restaurant". The building also served as a boarding house.

"The Frontenac Restaurant" was located next door to S. A. Rice's grocery store, in the 1940s and 1950s, and next to Victor and Harriet Holter's store until 1971, when Tomforde's residence/restaurant burned down.

Albert Tomforde died in 1981 and he and his two wives are buried in Oakwood Cemetery in Red Wing.

Service Stations, Garages and Auto Repair Shops

(North part of lot 7, Block 9)

Frontenac Garage ca. 1925. Three men in front of the Frontenac Garage: Ben Sauter is on the left, the man in the center is unknown, and George "Shorty" Possehl is on the right. The building on the far right is Peters Bros. Bar & Billiards and presently B. Wells bar.

Sauter's Garage 1920-1923
(Leo W. Sauter)

In 1920 Leo and Anna Sauter bought lots 5, 6, and 7 in block 9, from August and Mary Santelman and, the following year, Leo Sauter built a service garage and auto repair shop on the southeast corner of Scandinavia and Germania streets, on the northern part of lot 7. The building was constructed of colored tile, 40 by 50 feet (2,000 square feet), with storage for fifteen cars.

In 1922 Leo Sauter sold the southern half of lot 7 to Louis and Ed Peters for a bar and billiard business. Leo William Sauter died in 1923 at the age of forty-four.

Service Stations, Garages, and Auto Repair Shops

Photos of Vic Wiech, Ben Sauter, Earl "Weizel" Henning, Bill Johnson, and George (Shorty) Possehl. (Photo donated by Vic Wiech to the Florence Township History Center)

Frontenac Garage 1923-1925
(Ben Sauter)

After Leo Sauter's death, his brother, Ben, purchased lots 5, 6, and 7 in 1923, and took over his brother's service garage, and renamed it the Frontenac Garage. William Johnson, who had more than seven years' experience, was his auto mechanic.

Ben Sauter has a general repair business handling Goodrich tires, and made electrical repairs, as required. His garage carried gasoline, lubricating oil, hard grease, rack, and free air and water service were given to motorists. Mr. Sauter has a feed grinding business in connection with his service garage.

(1924 Lake City Graphic-Republican)

From 1940 to 1945, the garage building sat empty. Later, Mr. Kline used the building for small projects, and the building was later used for storage. Eventually, the building was purchased by Rick Ellingson and torn down to make a larger parking lot for the B. Wells bar.

Service Stations, Garages, and Auto Repair Shops

Tydol Service Station 1930
(Leonard Akeson)

Originally, US Highway 3 was paved in the Frontenac Station area in 1928, and after 1951, all of the gas pumps in town were removed to make way for the enlargement of US Highway 61.

By 1930 Leonard Akeson was managing a Tydol service station on the south side of the highway, across from August Santelman's grocery store. Later, the station changed to a Shell service station.

Leonard Akeson was born March 15, 1902, in Florence Township, the son of John and Mary (Larson) Akeson. In 1920 his siblings were: Edward A., Henry J., Edith L., Carl W., and George A.

Leonard married Mabel W. Akeson and they had two girls, Jeanne and Marilyn. (Marilyn would later operate Marilyn's Bar.) Leonard Akeson died June 11, 1962, and is buried in Oakwood Cemetery in Red Wing.

Wally Berlin Sr. and his son, Wally Jr. (Butch), sitting in front of their cycle shop, which they opened in 1961 in the former Frontenac State Bank building. (Notice the Italian Benelli and Capriolla motorcycles.) Berlin sold the business in 1984. (Photo courtesy of Butch Berlin)

Berlin's Cycle Shop 1961-1984
(Wally Berlin Sr. and Wally Berlin Jr.)

Service Stations, Garages, and Auto Repair Shops

Looking down US Highway 61, at Frontenac Station, in the 1940s. Edwin Bade's Shell service station is on the left and Sumner Rice's grocery store on the right, with Skelly gas pumps in front. Albert and Grace Tomforde's Frontenac Restaurant, was next door to Rice's grocery store. (Photo courtesy of Florence Township History Center)

Shell Service Station 1947-1956
(Edwin Bade)

Edwin Walter Bade was born in Lake City, November 14, 1893, to Henry E. and Adeline (Haase) Bade. Edwin married Elsie O. Palmer in 1916 and by 1930 they were farming in the Welch area. Their children were Mildred, Elenore, Agnes, Marion, Ethel, Robert, William, and Irene.

By 1940 the family had moved to Florence Township, where Edwin was doing farm and road work. In 1947 he succeeded Leonard Akeson in running the Shell service station on the south side of US Highway 61 at Frontenac Station. Edwin Bade died in 1965.

Service Stations, Garages, and Auto Repair Shops

Witt's Garage 1930-1935
(Edward C. Witt)

Ed Witt married Myrtle McKeen, daughter of Milton and Isabelle McKeen who was originally from Diamond Bluff, Wisconsin. In 1929 Ed and Myrtle purchased one half of lot 8 in block 6 and opened an auto repair shop which was located on the north end of Frontenac Station, on Highway 61.

In 1930 Ed and Myrtle rented the house next to the repair shop which was owned by Laura Franz. They shared their home with Myrtle's father and mother, Milton and Isabelle McKeen, Myrtle's two brothers, Ralph and Roy and Myrtle's Aunt Georgie.

By 1935 Ed and Myrtle had moved to Spring Valley, Wisconsin where Ed was self employed, possibly in another auto repair shop. Edward Charles Witt died in 1945. After Ed's death, Myrtle moved to Red Wing. In 1945 Charley Roper then took over Witt's Garage.

Milton and Isabelle McKeen and her sister Mary Hunter, sitting in front of the home they shared with their daughter and son-in-law, Ed and Myrtle Witt. Ed Witt's garage/repair shop is seen on the far right. The house is still at the original location but the shop was later demolished. Photo ca. 1930

Service Stations, Garages, and Auto Repair Shops

Left to right: Leslie McKeen, Earl Luckman, Roy McKeen, Ralph McKeen, Ed Witt, and Myrtle Witt

Roper's Repair Shop 1940-1970
(Charley Roper)

Charley Roper was born November, 1895 the son of Harvey and Louisa (Wohlers) Roper. He was one of eleven children; Henry, Fred, John, Harvey Jr., Charley, Alfred, Lorna, Mary, Doretha, Emma, and Alvera. (Charley's brother Henry was in the local community band , along with a Kuhfuss and Clarence Wiebusch).

As a young man, Charley worked on his father's farm when he got his arm caught in the threshing machine. However, this serious injury did not interfere with his occupation as an auto mechanic.

In 1940 Charley Roper married Mabel Jacobson and in 1945 Charley and Mabel purchased lots 7 and 8 in block 6 where Charley opened an auto repair shop, two blocks west of the Whistle Stop. The shop had formerly been operated by Ed Witt. Ropers lived in the house next to the repair shop which had once been the home of Ed and Myrtle Witt. Charley was a well known mechanic at Frontenac Station for many years. He died in 1970.

Vic's Auto Service 1947-1951
(Victor Wiech)

Vic's Auto Service building was built by Vic Wiech in 1947. Wiech worked at his service garage for three years and then sold it to Augustine & Baer in 1951.

Service Stations, Garages, and Auto Repair Shops

A popular landing area at Frontenac Station in the 1940s.

Donald Steffenhagen and others helped Harold Hoffman build Hoffman Aircraft. Donald's grandfather, Charles Hattemer, resided in Hay Creek Township (on County 2 Boulevard), where the workers put the parts together, brought them to Frontenac Station, and assembled parts of the aircraft in the basement of the Florence Town Hall. A popular landing area was in the vicinity of the former Discount Outlet store, across from the General Service Garage, where rides were given to the public.

(September 1996 Friends of the Florence Town Hall newsletter)

Clarence Peterson remembers when Bob Romek took flying lessons from Max Conrad, a well-known aviator from Winona. The plane took off and landed in the area of the Frontenac Outlet, next to US Highway 61. Viola Scherf, exiting the plane, jumped from the right side of the wing and was hit by the whirling propeller. She later died. Max Conrad was also injured by the propeller, in an attempt to catch Mrs. Scherf. After major head surgery at the Mayo Clinic in Rochester, Conrad survived.

Frontenac General Service 1951-1970
(M. C. "Al" Baer and Lenus Augustine)

When Baer and Augustine dissolved their partnership in 1970, Baer became sole owner.

Alvin and Evelyn Baer

Frontenac General Service

Motor Overhaul
Brake Repair
Welding
General Tractor and
Machinery Repair.

Also Mobilgas & Oil

A. C. "AL" BAER &
LENUS AUGUSTIN

Baer Garage & Repair 1970
(Al and Evy Baer)

Baer's residence was located in the rear of their repair business. Al Baer eventually sold his garage to Al Comstock and continued to work for him.

Service Stations, Garages, and Auto Repair Shops

Comstock Engineering
(Al Comstock)

Comstock was known as an inventor who developed a machine that would individually wrap products of all kinds.

Later, when Allison Heisler from Lake City bought Marilyn's Tavern in 1980, he also leased the Comstock engineering building across the street. This building would become a storage building for his merchandise at the new discount salvage store which he built at Marilyn's Tavern site.

(Photo courtesy of the Berlin family)

Berlin's Auto Repair
(Theodore "Ted" Berlin)

Theodore "Ted" Berlin bought the storage building from Gary Stiller in November 2006 and remodeled it for his auto repair shop.

Originally Schneider's tavern, now remodeled, and is a private residence.

Taverns, Bars and Saloons

Jacob Schneider's Tavern 1865-1872
Old Frontenac

Born in Germany in 1831, Jacob Schneider immigrated to America in 1851 and in 1856 married Dorothea Shale, who was also born in Germany. In 1858, they came to Goodhue County and settled in Old Frontenac. Schneider enlisted in the Seventh Minnesota infantry, Company G, in 1861 and served three years. Schneider returned to Goodhue County where he opened a store/tavern, in Old Frontenac. The tavern was one of the earliest buildings in Old Frontenac and later became the home of Evert Westervelt's grandson, Jamie Westervelt.

In 1872 Schneider bought land from Israel Garrard and moved to Frontenac Station, where he opened a grocery and provisions store, on what is now called Sclavonia Street, (lots 1 and 2 in block 12).

Taverns, Bars and Saloons

Albert Smith Tavern 1907
Location unknown

The 1907 Red Wing Directory stated that Albert Smith was a proprietor of a tavern at Frontenac, with George Smith as barkeeper.

There was also a mention, in the minutes of a town hall meeting, of Roper's tavern, in the 1870s (the location of this tavern is unknown).

During the days of Prohibition, the taverns at Frontenac Station were always packed, and one could get bootleg liquor any time, and stories tell of seven taverns at Frontenac Station during this time. (According to Evelyn Kiester, the route from Hastings to Wabasha was called "Bootleg Alley.")

According to Clarence Peterson, during the very early years, there were three taverns at Frontenac Station: one at the site of Dave and Shirley Sommerfield's house, another located at the earlier Berlin's Cycle Shop site, and the third, on Sclavonia Street where Krugers once lived (later the Bonde residence).

Photo taken in the early 1930s at the Minnesota State Fair. Left to right: George W. Kuhfuss - bass horn, Charles Kuhfuss - trombone, August Kuhfuss - trumpet, Herman Kuhfuss - clarinet, Garfield Kuhfuss - clarinet

Kuhfuss Bros. Band

Kuhfuss Nite Club 1932-1936
(Herman F. and Garfield [Gardy] Kuhfuss)

The tavern and dance hall was built by Herman Kuhfuss in 1932. It was located next to the Florence Town Hall on US Highway 61, and was run by father and son, Herman and Garfield Kuhfuss, who also ran a tavern in Bay City, Wisconsin.

August "Augie" Kuhfuss had a band that played at dances at Frontenac Station, as did his sister's band, the Dutch Masters, from Lake City.

The Kuhfuss Orchestra

The Kuhfuss Little German Band began in 1866. At the request of his two daughters in America, George A. Kuhfuss came to Minnesota from Germany where he had directed a 65-piece military band in Hannover. He and his family settled in West Albany, Wabasha County. His son, George E., studied music in Germany and became an accomplished violinist.

George E. Kuhfuss married Augusta Reinhardt of Minneiska, Minnesota. With his daughter and four sons, he organized a family band. George W. played the violin; Charlie played the trombone; Herman played the bass fiddle, clarinet, and saxophone; August (Augie) played the cornet and drums; and Augusta played the piano.

Their engagements took them throughout Wabasha and Goodhue counties and into Wisconsin, traveling by horse and buggy or sleigh, drawn by a pair of buckskin ponies. They carried with them all their instruments, including a piano tied to the back of their carriage. They played in town halls, opera houses, and farm barns, most of which are no longer standing.

In 1911 George Kuhfuss died, but the band continued under George W., the eldest son. The family now owned a Ford car and could return home after their nightly engagement.

When traveling with horse-drawn equipment, it was not uncommon for the entire band to be given room and board by the people who hired them. They played in Mazeppa, Gorman's Hall in Goodhue, Burkard's Hotel and Dance Hall in Hay Creek, and sometimes at Watson's barn.

About 1922, Herman and his family moved to Burnside, outside of Red Wing, where they held weekly barn dances in their own barn. (Their barn was located on US Highway 61, near the former County Poor Farm). Laws requiring permits, the stricter fire regulations, and the improved transportation facilities brought the barn dance era to an end. August, the youngest son, also went into nightclub entertaining. He was sometimes called the One Man Band, as he played the piano, drums, and trumpet all at one time.

After the death of George W., the Kuhfuss Orchestra continued to entertain, with Herman and his son, Gardy, managing the band. Now traveling by bus, they toured the entire Midwest.

(Goodhue County Historical News 1974 "Goodhue County's Early Orchestras")

Mr. and Mrs. Herman Kuhfuss and their two sons, Garfield and Verneil, moved to Rochester in 1938. The Kuhfuss Bros. band, while in Rochester, included the two brothers, Verneil and Garfield, their father, Herman, their uncle August, and from five to seven other musicians.

At various times, Verneil played with the Six Fat Dutchmen, Lynn Kern, Al Menke, Bennett Greten, and Skip Anderson Bands.

Forming another band was Mrs. Harry (Augusta Kuhfuss) Schmidt, daughter of George Kuhfuss. In 1942 she managed her own band in Lake City, which included her husband, two sons, and two daughters, and was known as the Dutch Masters.

(As told by Evelyn Kiester and 1952 Daily Republican Eagle)

An article in the Lake City Graphic-Republican stated that Charles and Herman Kuhfuss, of Millville, purchased the sample room of Kirsch & Ross of Lake City in 1917.

Taverns, Bars and Saloons

Hulvorson's Tavern 1939-1944
(Athel W. Hulvorson, owner)
(Fred and Cecile Reichert, managers 1944)

(Photo courtesy of Jean Dankers)

Shep's Tavern 1944-1948
(Francis and Helen Shephard, owners)
(M. L. Priebe, manager 1946-1948)

Francis (Shep) & Helen Shephard
(Photo courtesy of Jean Dankers)

DANCE
Saturday, Nov. 18
Shep's Tavern
Frontenac
Music by
Augie Kuhfuss

DANCE
Shep's Tavern
Frontenac
Saturday, Dec. 23
Music by
HIAWATHA VALLEY ORCH.

WEDDING DANCE
Barbara Holthe & Vic Shephard
FRIDAY, APRIL 11
Music by
Don's Rhythm Kings
SHEP'S
Frontenac

Taverns, Bars and Saloons

Ridgeway's Tavern 1948-1950
(Louis and Virgil Ridgeway) (father and son)

Ridgeway's Tavern 1950-1956
(Louis and Mary Ridgeway) (husband and wife)

Others that ran the bar were Edwin and Phyllis Selck 1956-1957, Carl Blakely 1957, and Robert and Pearl Lehman (Lehman's Bar) 1957-1967.

```
FREE
Wedding Dance
RIDGEWAY'S TAVERN
Frontenac, Minn.
SATURDAY, NOV. 25
Bette Ann Anderson -
Karl Blattner
Music by
MEL'S OLD TIMERS
```

Lehman's Bar 1957-1967
(Robert & Pearl Lehman)

Marilyn Akeson, left, with building-buyer Allison Heisler (Staff photo by Randy Johnson)

Marilyn's Tavern 1967-1980

(Marilyn Akeson)

Marilyn Akeson was the owner and operator of Marilyn's Tavern on US Highway 61 at Frontenac Station, next to the Florence Town Hall. She bought the bar from Bob and Pearl Lehman on September 6, 1967. She had worked for them for six years before buying the tavern. Marilyn had her residence in a small two-room section in the rear of the bar. Later she moved to a lot with a mobile home owned by Butch Berlin located at the rear of her tavern building.

Most of her clientele were Frontenac Station and Lake City people. She would start her day at 9 a. m. and would not get home until 2 a. m. She finally got tired of working eighteen-hour days and the stress of trying to keep the bar successful. The tavern, furniture, and appliances went up for auction and everything but the tavern was sold to Paul Anderson of Bay City, who was remodeling his new tavern, The Pines.

(1980 Republican Eagle, photo by Randy Johnson)

In May of 1980, Marilyn sold her tavern to Allison Heisler, a Lake City buyer, who demolished the tavern building and erected a new building for his discount store.

Taverns, Bars and Saloons

Photo most likely of Ed and Louis Peters and their father, Joe Peters, sitting in front of Peter Bros. Bar & Billiards. Leo Sauter's garage is on the far left, ca. 1922. (Photo courtesy of GCHS)

Peters Bros. Bar & Billiards 1922-1925
(Edward and Louis Peters, owners)
(presently B. Wells)

In 1922, brothers Edward F. and Louis Peters purchased Leo Sauter's confectionery store and remodeled the building for their bar and billiard business. The building was located on Scandinavia Street, behind Santelman & Hjermstad's grocery store.

Country Club 1925-1939
(Edward Peters, owner)

Edward Peters

Later, Edward Peters dissolved the partnership with his brother, took over the business, and became sole owner. The name of the bar was then changed to the Country Club. Over the years, there were various managers of the Country Club, under Peters' ownership.

Federal officers get bootleggers; William Peters, a proprietor of a soft drink parlor at Frontenac was arrested Sunday afternoon in a raid by prohibition officers. He was to appear at the federal office Monday for arraignment on charges of violating liquor laws. (June 1928) (There appears not to have been a William Peters in Frontenac at this time. Perhaps they meant Edward Peters, who was running a soft drink parlor.)

Edward F. Peters, a single man, was born in 1891 and died in 1976.

Taverns, Bars and Saloons

Left to right: Mildred Peterson, Vernon Peterson, Al ?, Ann Benson, Laverne ?, and Leona ? (Some last names have yet to be identified.) (Photo courtesy and in memory of Terry Benson)

Benson's Orchestra

This photo of Benson's Orchestra was taken by Monroe Benson at Welch Creek. Organized by Monroe and Ann Benson of Red Wing, the group was a well-known "old-time orchestra." This seven-piece orchestra played quite often at all the taverns at Frontenac Station during the 1930s.

> Benson's orchestra will entertain you at the Country Club at Frontenac Saturday and Sunday nights, Oct. 26 and 27. Come to a real Nite club and enjoy yourself.—Adv
> 10-27-m

> Suey's orchestra will entertain you at the Country Club at Frontenac Saturday night Nov. 2nd and Benson's orchestra Sunday night, Nov. 3rd.—Adv.
> 11-4-m

Taverns, Bars and Saloons

Country Club 1939-1943
(Sumner A. Rice, manager)

In 1939 Sumner Rice took over the management of the Country Club, where he and his wife, Mabel, also decided to prepare and sell food in their bar. They added a small addition onto the left side of the building to be used as a kitchen, and painted the kitchen orange and black, representative of the Chinese foods that they served. In 1943 Rice left the tavern business and decided to go into the grocery business, purchasing August R. Santelman's grocery store.

> **Announcing...**
> FORMAL
> **OPENING**
> of the
> **Country Club**
> FRONTENAC
> **SATURDAY NIGHT**
> **JULY 1ST**
> We also wish to inform you that the Country Club is now under new management.
> —"Lenny" Wiech, Proprietor
> Plan Now to Come to the Country Club for Your Evening of Fun for the 4th of July
> OPEN EVERY NIGHT

Country Club 1944-1945
(Lenny Wiech, manager)

In 1945 Ed Peters sold the Country Club bar to Lloyd and Evelyn Kiester.

Taverns, Bars and Saloons

(Photo courtesy of Evelyn Kiester)

**Cap's Country Club
1945-1950**

(Lloyd and Evelyn Kiester)

Lloyd and Evelyn Kiester

When Lloyd and Evelyn Kiester bought the Country Club bar from Ed Peters in 1945, they changed the name to Cap's Country Club, as "Cap" was Lloyd's nickname. The Kiesters added another addition on to Rice's previous addition, and they used both additions for their kitchen, living room, and bedroom. Lloyd and Evelyn also served food at their bar. In 1950 they sold the bar to Art and Lilian Wiech.

Taverns, Bars and Saloons

GRAND OPENING OF

Cap's Country Club

Formerly the Country Club
FRONTENAC, MINN.

FRIDAY, AUG. 10TH

FINE FOODS AND BEVERAGES

CHICKEN SERVED THE WAY YOU LIKE IT

Mr. and Mrs. Lloyd Kiester, Props.
Phone Red Wing 45-F-4

1945

DANCING
9 to 12 P.M.
FRIDAY, MAY 23

Entertainment by
"THE THREE DON'S"

CAP'S
COUNTRY CLUB

1947

WE PRESENT FOR
YOUR ENTERTAINMENT

The 3 Dons

Tonight and
Saturday Night

CAP'S COUNTRY CLUB
Frontenac

1948

We Extend a Cordial Invitation
to You and Yours to Celebrate Our

3rd Anniversary

FRIDAY, AUGUST 27

We wish to thank you one and all for your patronage during the past three years.

FREE BEER

Will Be Served from 7:30 to 9:30 P.M.

Also Entertainment by the 3 Dons

CAP'S COUNTRY CLUB

MR. AND MRS. LLOYD KIESTER, Props., Frontenac

1948

Taverns, Bars and Saloons

Art's Country Club 1950-1961

(Arthur and Lilian Wiech)

Arthur and Lilian Wiech bought Cap's Country Club from Lloyd and Evelyn Kiester in 1950 and the name was changed to Art's Country Club. As their son was growing up, Art and Lil decided that a nightclub was not the proper environment for children. They closed the bar and Lil prepared to part with a lot of the old belongings that she had inherited and purchased. Before she could advertise the items, tourists and passersby bought them all. Lil bought more items and sold them quickly and before she knew it, she was in the antique business.

DANKER'S ORCHESTRA

ART'S COUNTRY CLUB

Frontenac

Saturday, Nov. 25

Joe & Carrie

at

ART'S COUNTRY CLUB

Frontenac

Saturday, Nov. 18

Lil's Shop 1961-1975
(Lilian Wiech)

Justice in an Antique Shop

Art Wiech was elected constable in 1961 and Lil was appointed justice of the peace after the death of the incumbent. After finishing that term, Lil ran for election and won. Lil and Art made a rare team of law and order. If a law was broken, Art made the arrest on foot, because there was no police car. He would take the perpetrator to the justice of the peace, who just happened to be his wife. Offenders would find often themselves in Lil's Antique Shop.

The front two-thirds of the old and classically antique country store was devoted to antiques. The back third was home for Art and Lil. Casual observers were moved to remark about the old bar and back bar, running the length of the room. That was the only antique not for sale.

Preserving law and order was not a difficult job. Neighborly feuds and disagreements, unruly dogs, and noisy vehicles were the main sources of disorderly conduct, which seldom reached the "gavel and sentence" stage. Highway patrolmen sometimes brought in traffic violators, and both plaintiffs and defendants often returned to buy antiques.

Weddings yielded equally happy patrons. Some couples arrived to be married in the dining room and left with their car filled with enough antiques to set up housekeeping.

This antique shop/justice of the peace/constable arrangement had been a happy marriage for justice, business, and Art and Lil.

Taverns, Bars and Saloons

Photos and article from the St. Paul Pioneer Press.

Lil and Art Wiech set a good example for getting along with their neighbors. Behind the shop was a big barn. Art painted three-quarters of it barn red and called it his "Little Red Barn." The neighbors living behind the barn thought the red color too suggestive of a red barn, so Art painted the back wall white to blend in with the neighbor's color scheme. Of such compromises is law and order maintained at Frontenac Station.

(St. Paul Pioneer Press, June 11, 1967, donated courtesy of Shirley Sommerfield, Frontenac)

Art Wiech died of a heart attack while doing business at the Frontenac post office in 1975. Lilian Wiech sold her building to Larry Getchell, who remodeled it back to a bar, and from then on, it would be well known as B. Wells.

Constable Art, who recently broke his arm, does the police work.

Taverns, Bars and Saloons

James C. "Bully" Wells

James Wells was born at Gloucester, New Jersey in 1803. In 1819, at the age of fifteen, he enlisted in First United States Infantry, Company H, and came to Fort Snelling with Col. Henry Leavenworth, who established the post. Wells served for fifteen years and knew the northern wilderness, well. He was honorably discharged in 1834.

His first venture after leaving the army was to establish a trading post at Little Rapids, now known as Chaska, Minnesota.

Jane (Graham) Wells was born on St. Peter's River, Minnesota Territory, in 1804, the daughter of Duncan Graham and Susan Pennishon (Gray Huckleberry Woman), who was the granddaughter of Wapasha I, Chief of the Mdewakanton Sioux. She was thus a descendent of Opechancanough, brother of Powatan and uncle of Pocahontas.

(Information from North Dakota History in The James "Bully" Wells Collection #1 by Philip Faribault.)

Jane Graham married James Wells at Fort Snelling on September 12, 1836. To this union ten children were born: Sarah, Alfred, Orman, Mark, Elizabeth, William Wallace, Lucy, Aaron, Agnes, and Phillip. Jane was an expert marksman—supposedly better than her husband.

James Wells was a member of the legislative assembly of Minnesota Territory from 1848 to 1851. His associates called him "Bully," because of his habit of settling questions with his fists and arguing about them afterwards.

In 1837 he and his wife arrived at the future site of Frontenac, where Wells settled on the West bank of Lake Pepin. He set up a trading post in the bay, just above Point Au Sable. The riverboat pilots came to know the trading post, above Long Point, by its Dakota name, Waconia, and later, as Western Landing and later yet, as Bully Wells Bay.

Wells lived in a stone house, probably the first of its kind erected in any part of the territory, surrounded by a number of Dakota lodges belonging to his wife's relatives. Since Bully was married to a Dakota half breed, a daughter of Indian trader Duncan Graham, he was a deeded one hundred acres of land where he conducted his trading post for the next sixteen years.

(From the James "Bully" Wells Collection #1, by Philip Faribault Wells, donated by the Charles Davis Wells family to the Florence History Center)

It was not until 1851 or 1853 that the government began the tedious task of taking a census of all mixed blood Indians in the territory. By dividing the number of mixed blood natives into the number of total acres, the government determined each man, woman, or child would be entitled to 480 acres.

Taverns, Bars and Saloons

The Indians were issued "scrip" for the land. They could select any spot of land within the Half Breed Tract and claim it as their own. A federal land agent then filled in the Indian scrip and sent it to Washington DC. In return for the scrip, the Indians were granted official land patents.

Indian land rights in the Half Breed Tract ended in the 1860s. In 1862 Indians were banished to reservations and all land rights were relinquished.

(1975 Republican Eagle)

As a number of white settlers began streaming into Wells' area, in 1853 Bully Wells decided to leave. He had lived a long time among the Indians, but his relationships with his own race were sometimes far from harmonious, so he sold his buildings to Evert Westervelt.

In 1853 the Wells family moved to the foot of Wells Lake, Minnesota, and started a trading post, which was protected by a stockade made of oak timbers. The stockade was a square, log enclosure with an open space inside that protected the dwelling house, a store, and a storeroom.

In 1863 the Wells family moved again, to a site of what was then Okamon, Minnesota, where Wells opened a new trading post and remained there one year.

Homeseekers crowded into Rice County, where the Wells family lived before the Dakota War of 1862. This influx of new residents made James want to move out of the populated area. It was always his intention to establish a trading post in the Black Hills someday.

In 1864 he was en route to the Black Hills to confer with Yellow Bear about establishing a trading post. He took three of his boys with him, Wallace, seventeen, Aaron, eleven, and Phillip, thirteen. Instead of going due west, Wells took a route which ran near Spirit Lake, Iowa. He believed would avoid hostile Indians. A band of seemingly friendly Indians stopped Bully and Phillip's wagon. (Wallace and Aaron were back at their camp hunting elk.) They deliberately shot James in the head. Fortunately, Phillip escaped and made it back home. The three boys buried their father near the spot where he was killed.

(Information from the James "Bully" Wells Collection #1, by Philip Faribault Wells, donated by the Charles Davis Wells family to the Florence Township History Center)

Taverns, Bars and Saloons

B. Wells 1975-1980
(Larry Getchell)

The bar was named after Frontenac's first settler, James "Bully" Wells, fur trader and trapper.

Larry Getchell, a special education teacher in Lake City, decided both to teach and run a bar. First he had to remodel the building back to a bar from the former antique shop. During the winter months, the bar would be open only on weekends and evenings, with expanded hours in the summer.

(1976 Republican Eagle [photo also from newspaper)

Over the years the B. Wells bar had several owners, including William and Linda Alton, John and Arlene "Cookie" Serres, Steve and Karen Borgschatz, and partners, Brad Peterson and Rick Ellingson. Currently, Rick and Marge Ellingson are the owners.

Taverns, Bars and Saloons

Taverns on Sclavonia Street

In 1873 Israel Garrard sold lot 12 in block 11 to Jacob Schneider. In 1879 a building that had been constructed about 1864 in Old Frontenac was moved to Schneider's lot on Sclavonia Street. The building had always been used as a tavern and, in the early days, was a popular gathering place for residents of the community, where many problems dealing with local, county, and state affairs were discussed. Outside of the town hall, it was the only building where the public could meet, and especially under the management of its earlier owners, it was made available for this purpose.

Albert Schmidt acquired the building in 1895 and was owner until 1923, when he sold the business to Leo Sauter (presently the property of Mrs. Arland Adler).

Possibly Albert Schmidt's tavern. People behind the bar, possibly Leo Sauter, manager and bartender for Schmidt, and wife, Anna Sauter, and son, Raymond, ca. 1911.

Schmidt's Tavern 1895-1923

Albert Schmidt married Bertha Schenach on June 20, 1894. Albert and Bertha's first home was built as an extension of Schmidt's saloon on Sclavonia Street. There were three rooms downstairs and two rooms upstairs. There was a large room between the saloon and their living room, where the women could sit. (In the late 1890s and early 1900s, women who accompanied their menfolk to a saloon, did not go in; instead, they either stayed outside or went into another room and their drinks were brought to them). In the rear of the tavern was a small dance floor. In 1909 Harry H. Scherf was a bartender for Albert Schmidt.

Taverns, Bars and Saloons

Person unidentified, but possibly Leo Sauter behind the bar of his newly purchased, and updated tavern, ca. 1923, formerly Albert Schmidt's tavern.

Sauter's Tavern 1923
(Leo and Anna Sauter)

I believe Leo Sauter was the manager/bartender for Albert Schmidt between 1911 and 1920. In 1923 Leo Sauter purchased Albert Schmidt's bar on Sclavonia Street but, unfortunately, Leo died that same year at the age of forty-four. Anna Sauter took over the bar and later she and her son, Raymond, leased the bar to various managers over the years. Anna later married Fred Possehl.

Alpers Bar & Billiards 1924-1926
(Anna and son, Raymond, Sauter, owners)
(John Alpers, manager)

According to the 1924 *Red Wing Directory,* John Alpers was operating a soft drink parlor (tavern). The tavern, formerly the Albert Schmidt tavern, was located on Sclavonia Street. John's son, Ernest, went to work at his father's soft drink parlor in 1924, staying there until opening a confectionery store.

John Alpers was born in Hannover, Germany, in 1859. He married Dora Mieners in 1886 in Germany. The couple came to the United States in 1892 with their children Heinrich (Henry), Cathrina, and Ernest and in 1910 resided in Hay Creek. By 1920 their family had moved to Florence Township, where John farmed. By 1924 Alpers was operating a soft drink parlor, formerly Sauter's tavern.

John Alpers died January 7, 1941, leaving two sons, J. Henry Alpers and Frank Alpers; (another son Ernest was already deceased), five daughters, Mrs. L. A. Fellman, Mrs. Roy Paton, and Mrs. W. J. Alpers, all of Red Wing, Mrs. R. A. Paton of Austin, and Katherine Alpers, at home.

Taverns, Bars and Saloons

Lemke Nite Club 1932-1935
(Anna Sauter Possehl and Ray Sauter, owners)
(Louis Lemke, manager)

In 1932 Louis Lemke moved to Frontenac Station and leased the tavern owned by Annie (Sauter) Possehl and her son, Raymond. Lemke named the tavern the Lemke Nite Club.

Louis Lemke was born in 1883 in Wabasha County. He stayed on the farm until he was twenty years old and then moved to Mazeppa. He became branch manager of the clothing store of L. E. Sigmond of Zumbrota. Lemke also operated the Lemke General Store in Mazeppa for four years and also served as marshal of Mazeppa for seven years. By 1925 he was part of the real estate firm of Reiland and Lemke at Mazeppa, which business he was in for about seven years. Louis Lemke died in 1935.

Pederson's Tavern 1939
(Anna Sauter Possehl & Ray Sauter, owners)
(Alfred Pederson, manager)

Frontenac Family Routed By Early Morning Blaze

Three boys had narrow escapes from serious injury or possible death and one suffered a bad burn on one of his feet in a fire which destroyed what is known as the old Schmidt saloon building at Frontenac this morning.

Lindy 9, who was asleep downstairs suffered severe burns to his right foot as he was forced to run through burning embers and flames to reach safety. Joe, 15, and Jense, 13, who were upstairs, got out in the nick of time. Jense jumped from as second-story window and Joe made his way down a smoked-choked and smoldering stairway to safety, helping his younger brother out of the building.

The injured youth was rushed to the Lake City doctor's office by Earl Luckman of Frontenac. The boy was able to return to Frontenac that same day.

The fire was discovered by the man on duty at the Leonard Akenson oil station on highway 61 across the tracks from the Schmidt building. His cries of "fire" attracted Alfred Pederson, father of the boys, who was sitting on the lawn outside the building waiting the boiling of a pot of coffee that he had placed on an oil stove which he had lighted in the kitchen a short time before.

The father rushed to the structure which had almost instantly been turned into a burning inferno. He called to his sons who were still asleep. They were quickly awakened and made their escape without outside help.

The building was owned by Mrs. Anna Sauter Possehl. The Pederson's lost everything with the exception of a few articles of clothing which the boys grabbed when they fled. The Lake City fire department was called but by the time they arrived, the entire building was all in flames. The fire fighters and volunteers then devoted their efforts to saving a barn on the adjoining property, owned by Mrs. Possehl but leased by Arthur Gerken.

Taverns, Bars and Saloons

The building was one of the oldest in the Frontenac community. Old-timers say it was constructed close to seventy-five years ago (1879) and had been removed from Old Frontenac to its present location over sixty years ago (1894). It had been operated practically all the time since then as a tavern, first by the late Albert Schmidt. Others who conducted a business there were the late Louis Lemke and Leo Sauter, Mr. Pederson and others. It had been closed for several weeks past, but the living quarters were occupied by the Pedersons.

In the early days the tavern was a popular gathering place for residents of the community and here many problems dealing with local county and state affairs were discussed and decided after heated debates. Outside of the town hall it was the only building where the public could meet. When the flames had died down all that remained of the large frame building were a few smoldering ashes and posts of what was once the porch.

(1939 Daily Republican)

Landmark Destroyed by Fire; 3 Escape

Fire, which started from a coffee pot boiling over, completely demolished one of the oldest buildings in Frontenac, at about seven o'clock this morning. The building which was moved from old Frontenac to the present site over sixty years ago is best remembered by old timers as the Albert Schmidt saloon. It had always been used as a tavern and was located directly across the tracks from the oil station operated by Leonard Akenson. The ruins were still smoldering when The Daily Republican cameraman took the above picture shortly after 8 a. m.

The rear and upstairs of the tavern at Frontenac destroyed by fire this morning was occupied by the Alfred Pederson family. Mr. Pederson is shown holding his son Lindy, 9, who had his right foot burned in escaping from the building. Joe, 15, at the left escaped by the stairway while Jense, 13, left himself drop from a second story window.

Taverns, Bars and Saloons

The Hillside Inn

(Bar/Restaurant)

The bar/restaurant was located on Sclavonia Street, possibly at the former Haustein & Schmidt Grocery and Provision Store site. Photo looks to be in the 1920s or 1930s. (Hillside Inn business card courtesy Gary Schumacher)

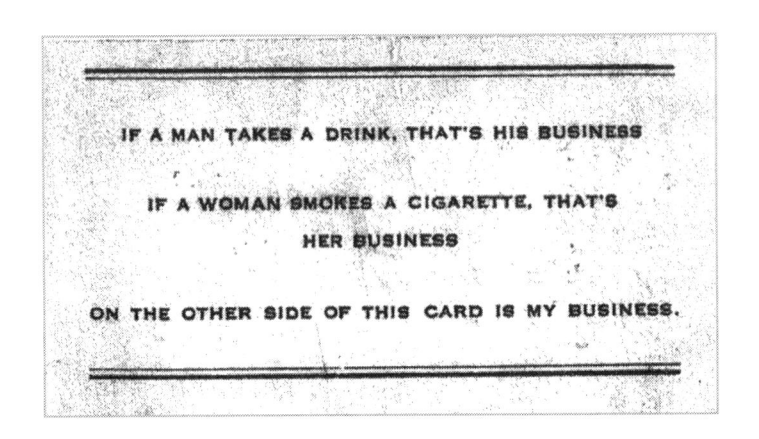

IF A MAN TAKES A DRINK, THAT'S HIS BUSINESS

IF A WOMAN SMOKES A CIGARETTE, THAT'S HER BUSINESS

ON THE OTHER SIDE OF THIS CARD IS MY BUSINESS.

HILLSIDE INN

DANCING .. BEER .. LUNCH

FRONTENAC, MINN.

> NOTICE TO
> PEOPLE OF FRONTENAC
> Due to circumstances beyond my control. I will be unable to make house-to-house delivery with ice. However, I will make one-stop trip on Monday, Wednesday and Friday evenings between 6 and 7:30 p. m. at Shell Oil Station.
>
> M. A. TORKELSON
> Parkway Service Station
> Red Wing   *1947*

The Frontenac Ice Company and Stockyards

The Frontenac Ice Company 1911-1940

It is not known who actually built this ice house, but it served this purpose until 1940.

After Lloyd and Evelyn Kiester purchased the Country Club from Ed Peters in 1945, they bought the two adjoining lots. The ice house was located on one of these lots, which was located to the left of their bar. Originally, the hole in the ice house floor was about six feet deep and the ice was then packed in sawdust, three feet deep.

The ice house sat empty for five years before the Kiesters turned the building into a garage. They bought two-inch planks from the Carlson Lumber Company and put a floor in the ice house, which made it suitable for their garage and storage.

The ice house building is still standing today, next to the B. Wells bar, which is now owned by Rick and Marge Ellingson.

According to the advertisement in the Red Wing newspaper, in the 1940s M. A. Torkelson, located at the Parkway Service Station in Red Wing, delivered ice, house to house, at Frontenac Station.

The Frontenac Ice Company and Stockyards

Ice Harvesting

Ice harvesting in Frontenac, prior to 1925

From about 1850 to 1940, ice was harvested each winter when it was at its thickest and, in Goodhue County, this occurred in late January. The blocks were used in stores and restaurants as well as in ice boxes, early refrigeration in family kitchens. The harvest lasted only two weeks. Farmers found that it put extra money in their pockets, at ice harvesting time, to hire out their teams, which were not needed on the farm. In Frontenac, visitors to the Lakeside Hotel could watch the harvest from front porches.

Once an area was squared up, a double-runnered tool, called an ice plow, was used to cut the ice. One of the runners served as a guide marker; it would run along a string that had been used to square up the surface. The cutting blade was on the second runner, and two horses pulled the ice plow, with a man walking behind to guide it.

(Photos and information from the Red Wing Republican Eagle Progress Edition, written by Ruth Nerhaugen)

The Frontenac Ice Company and Stockyards

A block from one of the floats was 22 by 32 inches. Depending upon the thickness, it weighed three hundred to five hundred pounds. The first piece taken out, called the "corner cake," usually was broken up, then the rest of the blocks were moved up a chute onto a loading platform, then to a sleigh or truck for transportation.

Natural ice harvesting peaked in the 1920s. Electric refrigeration was only one of the reasons, however. Industrialization was causing increasing stream and river pollution, and the Minnesota Board of Health began regular inspections to ensure that consumers were getting clean ice.

(Photos and information from the Red Wing Republican Eagle Progress Edition, written by Ruth Nerhaugen)

The Stockyards ca. 1919

Market day at Frontenac Station, where farmers came to town to buy, sell, or trade livestock, and also ship their livestock to various locations. The area for the sales always took place south of the railroad tracks, directly across from the Frontenac State Bank and the Gabe residence.

Frontenac Livestock Shipping Association

The shipping association was organized in 1923, with 160 farmer stockholders. Anton Schafer was president, Earl G. Hennings secretary, and Peter Cordes treasurer. The board of directors consisted of John P. Damman, John Alpers, and F. J. Huneke.

In 1923 they shipped fifty cars of livestock. By the next year, the shipping association was a growing organization at Frontenac Station, and a noticeable feature of its business was the interest taken in and the patronage given by the people of the surrounding community and trade territory.

Feed Building

Originally, a feed building was located in the alley, behind the present Whistle Stop. It was a long, narrow, open-front building with mangers and feed boxes for feeding the horses of farmers coming into town to do business. Farmers would tie their horses at the feed building, as it took some farmers all day to get to Frontenac Station and get back home.

Stock Pens

As you enter Frontenac Station the stock pens were located on the corner of US Highway 3, and County Road 2. Farmers would bring their livestock and put them in holding pens, while waiting to load them onto railroad cars for shipment to Chicago.

Hobo Camp

Later, the stock pen area became a camp for traveling hobos. They would go door-to-door, begging for vegetables and meat, bring the food back to the camp, and cook the food.

The Lubeck Stable 1911

John and William Lubeck were living at Rural Route 1, Frontenac, as early as the 1875 state census.

William and John Lubeck are busily engaged in the erection of a large stable, which, when completed will be a model building of its kind and a credit to two of Frontenac's most faithful and industrious young men.

(1911 Lake City Graphic) (Location unknown)

Warehouse 1871

(Murray Bros.)

The Murray Bros. have erected a warehouse at Frontenac Station, near the railroad. The purpose is to purchase or store grain, as may be desired.

(August 1871 Lake City Sentinel)

Frontenac Sash & Blind Factory 1867

On February 9, 1867, a sash and blind factory was built in Frontenac and the machinery was already on the ground, getting ready for use.

(1867 Lake City Graphic-Republican) (Location unknown)

Frontenac Lumber Mill 1868

(J. C. Read)

J.C. Read, owner of the Frontenac Lumber Mills had 70,000 feet of logs in his boom that he would saw as soon as he could get help, after the farmers were through with harvest.

(1868 Lake City Sentinel) (Location unknown)

The Frontenac Ice Company and Stockyards

Carlson Lumber Company 1920-1947
(Ray Carlson)

The Carlson Lumber Company was located on the east side of Frontenac Station, above Frontenac Pond. They specialized in particular kinds of lumber and sawed lumber for a furniture factory in St. Paul.

According to Vic Wiech, he worked at the sawmill for three years and also drove the lumber truck.

The First Sawmill Was Established in 1857 at Central Point 1857-1920s
(A. B. Grannis)
(G. H. Grannis)

A. B. Grannis was the original owner of the Central Point sawmill. In 1857 a partnership was formed among C. M. Lewis, Joseph Scott, and James W. Crawford. As his share of the firm, Lewis put in a locomotive engine, valued at $2,000. Each of the other men advanced $2,000 in cash.

The engine was brought from Alleghany to Central Point by river steamer at a cost of $671. Other supplies came up the river by steamers, the War Eagle, the Chippewa, and the Rocket.

Later, G. H. Grannis, father of A. B. Grannis, became owner of the mill, and a brother, S. S. Grannis became a partner for a time. Little business was done during the Civil War.

The firm handled a side line of groceries and flour and took wheat in payment for goods.

Stove wood was not worth much as, in 1870, a half cord was sold by the firm for thirty-eight cents.

(1924 Graphic-Republican)

The mill was torn down in 1920s.

The Frontenac Ice Company and Stockyards

Armour Company Lumber Sheds 1924

The Armour Company has some fine buildings at Frontenac, including extensive lumber sheds, with a spur track from the C. M. & St. Paul [Milwaukee Railroad] main line.

(1924 Lake City Graphic-Republican)

According to the photo, it looks like the lumberyards were located approximately in the same location as the former Frontenac Stone Company, but on both sides of County Road 2 as you cross the railroad tracks.

In 1927-1928 the lumber yard at Frontenac Station was sold to the two Cordes brothers, who tore down the buildings and salvaged the lumber to build a dance hall at Wells Creek.

The only pavilion for dancing erected in Goodhue County was the typical barn-shaped Wells Creek Dance Gardens, located in a grove of trees in a park along Wells Creek at the junction of county roads 2 and 5, near Beckmark's Corner. Charles Cordes purchased the land from John Possehl and had a 40 by 100-foot wooden structure built in the late 1920s. Dances were held in the upper level and the ground floor contained the lunch stands. Henry Roper and Robert Terwilliger managed the operations for several years and booked the famous Whoopee John and Ely Rice orchestras, as well as the local dance bands. The building then stood vacant until Jack Lowery and a Mr. Wilson had it dismantled in 1946-1947. The dimension lumber was used in building the Terrace at Lake City and the flooring became the dance floor of the Anchor Inn.

(Goodhue County Historical News, "Goodhue County's Early Orchestras")

Early Businesses On Top Of The Hill

In 1874 Nils (Nels) Carstenson, William Menke, E. Ackerman, H. Lorentzen and A. H. Keye all owned land on top of the hill, which is now 305th Street.

Hoffman Turkey Farm

Harold and Florence Hoffman had a turkey farm, located on what is now 305th Street close to the present gravel pit. Harold was one of three children of John and Minnie Hoffman, who had a farm located on County Road 2 near Frontenac Station.

Samuelson Turkey Farm 1960

The Samuelson turkey farm was the successor to the Hoffman turkey farm. (Ralph Samuelson was the man that invented water skiing.)

Geisler Hog Farm 1970

The Geisler hog farm was located on 305th Street next to the Lake City Airport. Some of the remains of the building are still at that site.

Race Track (County Road 2)

A mile-long race track built by the Garrard brothers (Israel and Jeptha) was located west of what was then called the military road, in Claus Meyer's pasture, which presently, would be next to the Frontenac Sportsman's Club, on County Road 2.

We learn that Gen. Garrard, of Frontenac, took a 2nd premium on a full blooded, 2 year old colt at the St. Louis fair. He has some of the finest blooded horses in the State and is fixing up a driving park on his premises at Frontenac, which when finished, will not be excelled in any place. This will greatly add to the interest of that place.
(1870 Wabasha County Sentinel)

Races were organized during the summer months and in 1872 there was a race between Ben McLean's horse Glencoe and Gen. Garrard's horse Red Oak. Red Oak won. Gen. Garrard had twenty-two race horses at the time of his death in 1901.

There was a mile long race track in 1878 at Dakota Park.
(History of Goodhue County Minnesota, 1878)

According to Alice Tackaberry, race horses were brought by boat from Missouri to Old Frontenac and were then raced at a racetrack on County Road 2, just past the Sportsman's Club. According to Naomi Roper, in the late 1930s or early 1940s, her parents would take her to see the races. The land now belongs to the Possehl family.

The Frontenac Ice Company and Stockyards

Bicycle Path 1890

As yet the bicycle club has not yet held its annual meeting nor has anything been done in regard to repairing the path between here and Frontenac. If it is the intention of the club to maintain this path, the work ought to be commenced at once.
(April 17, 1890 Red Wing newspaper)

Wm. Liewellyn has charge of the construction of the bicycle path between Red Wing and Lake City. At present he is employing a force of thirteen men.
(1897 Republican)

In 1897 a bicycle path was built between Red Wing and Lake City at a cost of $1,000 and with a lot of protest of bicyclists frightening horses.

This building is located on Pat Possehl's property, but it is not certain what this building had been used for. She felt the stone used in this building probably came from Tostevin's stone quarry.

Outdoor Movies

It was a big deal to come to Frontenac Station for movies in the 1950s. The screen was set up between Rice's grocery store and Cap Kiester's Country Club Bar (now B. Wells).

The local businesses sponsored the movies. After the movies were over, the children would have fun running around the neighborhood, while adults relaxed and visited with friends.

(Reported by Diane Ableidinger and Evelyn Kiester)

Tackaberry Game Farm

After Roy "Tac" Tackaberry had a stroke, his wife, Alice, decided they needed some kind of hobby to keep them both active. She joined the Pheasant & Waterfowl Society. She proceeded to go into the woods on her property and, by herself, dug post holes and put in posts and wire pens for the birds. She purchased rare birds from game farms and began to breed and raise rare birds that would otherwise be extinct in coming years. One breed she raised was Mille Fleurs, an ornamental bantam chicken, which she bred and then sold the offspring.

Later Alice bred and raised the white arctic fox. Her pet fox, Muffy, was her favorite. She had three breeding pair of foxes and she would later sell the offspring to families for pets. After a few years, the job of raising foxes got to be too much for Alice and she decided to give up the business.

(Information given by Alice Tackaberry)

The Local News

About 1857, David Kelly laid out a farm on the site of the present Frontenac Station when that place was little more than a wilderness. Afterwards, he lived for many years in Red Wing where he conducted the Kelly House (Hotel) on Plum Street. Mr. Kelly's place was the leading hotel of the town, during that time.
(1892 Advance Sun)

While engaged preventing a stampede of his cattle, Charles Hines, a farmer living near Frontenac Station, was attacked by a bull and fatally gored. One of the horns of the animal penetrated the bowels and left lung, He lived but a few hours.
(1880 Lake City Review)

A wreck occurred on the railroad two miles west of Frontenac Station at a point where the road makes a sharp curve. Four cars, belonging to No. 12 freight were thrown from the track. The track was smashed and not passable for six hours, which delayed the eastbound passenger No. 4. The occasion of the wreck was a side board of a coal car falling off the rails. Earlier, conductor No. 8 fired three seedy looking tramps off of his train who had been stealing a ride in the box cars. In retaliation, the three men accosted John Anderson who took care of the Florence cattle. Then they headed for the Russell & Son Mill, where they stole a boat and supplies. They paddled over to the Wisconsin side of the lake, but were soon caught near Winona. One of the men was notorious and wanted in Nebraska.
(1880 Lake City Review)

Married, at the residence of Mr. Tomfohr, in Frontenac, Fred Tomfohr to Miss Regina Wegrich, both of Frontenac. They intend on moving to Red Wing with the intention of engaging in the bakery business.
(1887)

Frontenac is enjoying a small sized building boom at present.
(1887)

Married at the Episcopal rectory, last Tuesday, at 4 p. m., Rev. C. H. Plummer officiating, Charles Savage and Emma Martinson, both of Frontenac.
(1887 Advance Sun)

The game of baseball between the Lake City Lightfoots and Kelly's Colts of Frontenac, resulted in an overwhelming victory for the Lightfoots by a score of 50 to 9. The features of the game were the batting of the Lightfoots, the errors of the Frontenac's and Kelly's kicking.
(1889 Lake City Republican)

Frontenac has a militia company of about thirty members, with Will Savage, as captain.
(1889 Republican)

The Local News

In 1904 Edward F. Huneke grew plum trees and sold plums for five cents a piece in Red Wing. In 1911 he was also the constable.
(1904)

H. L. Curry of Frontenac, has sold over $600 worth of strawberries this season.
(1891 Advance Sun)

The trouble at Frontenac over liquor selling without a liquor license is but the forerunner of general warfare against these illicit liquor sellers.
(June 1893)

J. J. Doughty moved from Lake City to Frontenac, where he will engage in the grain buying business.
(1892 Advance Sun)

In 1895 John Peters of Frontenac bought an interest in the saloon business of Henry Schulenberg of Red Wing, at 212 Plum Street.

Several car loads of material for the electric light and power company were shipped to this point during the past two weeks. We have been informed that it is the intention of the company to put in a transformer opposite the station and extend the lines to the Inn and Villa Maria which would add considerable to the revenue of the company inasmuch as both places would require a large number of lights.
(1911 Lake City Graphic)

The home of Ben Santelman was struck by lightning Monday night and a considerable amount of damage was done to the house.
(1914)

Division Engineer, William Geisheker reports the near collapse of the old wooden bridge below Frontenac, when a team, drawing a heavy load of gravel, passed over it. The big wooden span sagged over a foot in the center and for a time it was feared that the entire structure would fall with a crash. Temporary repairs were made at once. The double 45 foot girder span bridge of reinforced concrete is now under construction below Frontenac, and will be open to traffic within the next five or six weeks.
(1914)

A new bridge is being erected on the Frontenac-Lake City road near the Kingsley home. The old structure was set at an angle with difficult approaches and had been in a weakened condition for some time. Motorists, especially, will welcome the improvement.
(1917)

The Local News

Frontenac Farmer Commits Suicide

After first trying to shoot his wife and then going to neighbor Ben Santelman, a Frontenac farmer, and attempting to kill him, Edward Herder, aged about fifty years, went into his own home at Frontenac, locked all the doors and windows, laid down on a bed in the bedroom and placed a revolver close to his left breast and pulled the trigger.

Herder lived on a farm between Old Frontenac and New Frontenac. His wife and 16-year-old daughter left him because of his quarrelsome nature. He went to Old Frontenac where his wife was staying and aimed a revolver at her, but she escaped. He then went over to the Ben Santelman farm and approached Mr. Santelman, who was hitching up a horse gang plow, and did not notice him. When he turned around, Herder was aiming to shoot him, but the gun did not go off. Santelman got away and ran to Frontenac to call the sheriff. By the time the sheriff got to Herder's house, Herder was already dead with a self-inflicted gunshot to the breast.

(1918 Lake City Republican)

The Red Wing Sporting Goods basketball team defeated the newly organized Frontenac team, at Frontenac, by a score of 40 to 12. The Frontenac five were slow in getting started and the Red Wing team piled up a 20 to 4 lead during the first quarter. Peterson was the heavy scorer for Frontenac, dropping in three field goals. Akenson got the other one for the losers. Possehl shot two out of four fouls for Frontenac. "Wink" Esterly, of Red Wing, who refereed the game, said that Frontenac had the makings of a mighty good team, and continuous practice would bring them to the front.

(1921 Graphic-Republican)

At the annual meeting of the Frontenac Shipping Association, Wm. Scherf was elected manager in place of Albert Schmidt, who had been manager for several years. President was Antone Schafer, secretary, Harvey J. Roper Sr., treasurer, Harry Lewis, directors John Damman, John Alpers, and Fred Wohlers.

(1920 Graphic-Republican)

Edward Peters, son of Mr. and Mrs. J. Peters of Frontenac, returned from overseas Monday. He left for Camp Dodge, September 19, 1917, and went to France in June of last year. While in France, he served with the 123rd Field artillery and saw considerable active service at the front.

(1919)

Hog cholera exists in the township of Florence. All persons owning dogs are hereby notified to tie them up. Observe all other precautions as required by law governing such contagious diseases. Ed Schmidt, chairman.

(1931)

A fox and coon chase, sponsored by local sportsmen and the Winona Coon Club, will be held at the Ray Carlson home, one and one half miles from Frontenac Station, Sunday, beginning at 10:30 a. m. All interested are invited to attend and those with dogs are asked to bring them.

(1937)

The Local News

Richard Grimm, 62-year-old Florence Township farmer, lost all but the little finger on his right hand when it was drawn into the mechanism of a silo cutter at his farm Saturday afternoon. Grimm was feeding corn into the cutter when the accident occurred. The sharp knives made a diagonal cut across the hand above the knuckles. It was necessary to amputate.

(1944)

Charles Berg of Red Wing and I. G. Munger of Frontenac were engaged in a game of billiards when an altercation over some matter arose between the two. In a moment of passion, Munger took a billiard cue and struck Berg over the head, inflicting an ugly wound about three inches long and a half an inch wide. Berg has sworn out a warrant for the arrest of Munger.

The row at Frontenac on Monday, which resulted in the wounding of Charles Berg, and caused the arrest of I. G. Munger, has stirred up things and precipitated a legal attack upon parties at that place selling liquors without a license.

M. Ackerman appeared before the justice of the peace this morning and swore out three warrants. I. G. Munger of Frontenac, was brought to Red Wing and appeared before Justice Diepenbrock, charged with assault on the person of Chas. Berg with a billiard cue.

It is stated by people from Frontenac, that there has been much feeling in that vicinity recently over the alleged open manner in which blind pigs have been conducted, but no one has apparently dared to swear out warrants for the arrest of the guilty parties.

The warrants sworn out in justice court by M. Ackerman were against Charles Scherf, who was employed in the store of Casper Haustein, and John Larson, who has been in the employ of Lorenz Hoffman. There were two complaints against Scherf and one against Larson for selling liquor without a license.

The sheriff went to Frontenac to serve the warrants. Charles Scherf was arrested, but John Larson, who had gotten a scent of what was being done, had left for parts unknown. The prosecution believes it has a strong case and that a wholesome lesson will be taught the unlicensed liquor dealers at Frontenac.

(1893)

Thieves operated at Frontenac the first of last week. They broke into Ed Huneke's tool shop and Carsten Bros. place, carrying away tools and cooking utensils to the value of about $50.

(1894 Advance Sun)

The Local News

John Mues has resigned his position as depot agent here, and expects to start a restaurant in Red Wing about the middle of the month.
(1894 Advance Sun)

J. H. Mues, for a number of years station agent of the Milwaukee road at Frontenac, has resigned and will engage in the confectionery business in Red Wing, at 220 Bush street.
(1894 Advance Sun)

The county commissioners have granted liquor license to C. J. F. Haustein of Frontenac.
(Advance Sun)

Frontenac merchants have changed from a credit to strictly cash business.
(1894 Advance Sun)

Florence Township has elected the following delegates to the Republican county convention: A. H. Mitchell, Ed Ackerman, John H. Mues, Wm. Paton, H. D. Norton and L. P. Forman.
(1894 Advance Sun)

The stacks of barley which were consumed by fire at Herman Scherf's place in Frontenac contained about 500 bushels of the best barley. The fire originated from sparks from the threshing engine. The grain was insured.
(1894 Advance Sun)

Art Munger was the Captain of the Frontenac Baseball Club in 1894.
(Advance Sun)

Wm. Munger is in a town working for a telephone company. His wife has started a boarding house in Minneapolis.

Killed in Frontenac

November 1, 1893, Isaac G. Munger was killed by the eastbound Milwaukee train which arrived in Frontenac at 9:45. It is supposed that he threw himself in front of the train. He was seen walking up the track and was killed in front of the stone mill; he was cut up in pieces, some of which were picked up sixty feet from where he was struck. His skull was left in his hat. He was killed within seventy-five yards of his own home. He left a wife and three children.

There were two cases against Munger in the district court. One charge was for assault, which occurred against Charles Berg of Frontenac. The other case was a civil action for damages to the amount of $2,800 for injuries sustained in the above mentioned trouble.

The principle witnesses were Mrs. W. E. Herlinger and Herman Scherf who were present and saw the ghastly spectacle. Their testimony went to show that the deceased could not have possibly been sane when he committed the act.

He was seen to run zig-zag up the railroad tracks and acting strangely. Probably because of the pending charges that preyed on his mind plus he being traced back to a "Blind Pig," might have been the cause of his tragedy.

(1893)

The health officers in Florence Township are evidently not going to put their light under a bushel, when they identify a contagious disease within their jurisdiction. There was four malignant cases of diphtheria in one family. About a half mile from the house was one red flag, a few rods from the house was another red flag and on the door was the usual sign reading "Contagious disease, diphtheria."

(1893 Advance Sun)

In 1893 a trial was up before Justice Tandy. There were two defendants, Carl Strupe and his little son, Albert Strupe. They were charged with assault and battery, the injured person being Mrs. Augusta Possehl, whose face showed traces of a conflict.

Charles Berg was secured as an interpreter to transfer [translate] German into English. Mrs. Possehl testified that Carl Strupe, and his son Albert, drove their cows past her home, when Albert jumped over the fence and began to attack the two Possehl boys. The mother tried to intercede, when Carl and his son became irate. Carl wielded a large birch branch at Mrs. Possehl and also hit her in her left eye. Albert hit her in the right eye, smashing her glasses. Carl was found guilty and paid a fine of $29.04 and the case against Albert Strupe was dismissed.

(1893 Advance Sun)

Morehouse Bros. of Frontenac, with a horse-power threshing machine, recently threshed for Englebert Schenach, 787 bushels of wheat in nine hours' time.

(1885 Graphic-Republican)

In 1912 Frontenac vs. Old Town, (Old Frontenac) with Frontenac winning 18 to 2.

The Silver Stars of Lake City vs. the Frontenac Juniors. The Juniors won 23 to 4.

In 1911 The Frontenac Daisy Club met, with Maude Schmidt in charge.

The Frontenac Cubs defeated the East Side Pickets, of Red Wing, by a score of 14 to 9. Clifford pitched a great game, striking out 17 of the Picket's batmen. This was one of the most exciting games this season.

(1914)

The Frontenac Terrors defeated the Belvidere All-Star Basketball team, at the Frontenac town hall, by a score of 44 to 13. Vollmers of this city was one of the shining lights for the winners with 6 field baskets and 2 free throws to his credit. Possehl, of Frontenac, caged 8 baskets and Alpers helped with 6 baskets.

(1923)

The Local News

Florence Farmer Killed by Train

Samuel I. Church, 47 years old, a farmer from near the town of Florence, was killed by a west bound train while going from his house to a meeting in Frontenac. He was walking with his brother, C. L. Church, when a train was coming. His brother climbed the bank to avoid the train, but Samuel must have been blinded by the lights etc. and was killed. The brother did not realize this and went on to the meeting and thinking his brother went somewhere else. The body was discovered the following day. Samuel Church lived with his brother on the farm which the two of them operated. He was buried at the Wacouta Cemetery.

(1917 Graphic-Republican)

Ray Sauter left for Minneapolis where he will join an orchestra which will leave soon for Seattle, from where they will sail on an ocean liner for the Philippine Islands. They expect to play in several cities along the way. The orchestra will play regular engagements on the boat. Mr. Sauter expects to be gone three months.

(1935 Lake City Graphic-Republican)

Florence Farmer Slain by Bull

Charlie Franz Weed's death resulted from an attack by a vicious bull on the farm home of his sister, Mrs. Fred Kingsley, with whom he lived.

Mr. Weed was born in Central Point Township, Goodhue County, January 24, 1863. He was the oldest son of David T. and Mary Northfield Weed, pioneer residents of the county. For many years, he conducted farming operations in North Dakota, living there 34 years. He was twice married. Following the death of his first wife, Anna Heggie of Florence, in 1900, he took up land near Minot. His second marriage to Fannie Routzhon of Maryland, also a North Dakota homesteader, took place in 1902. She died in 1932, and in 1934, upon the death of his brother-in-law, Fred Kingsley, he returned to Minnesota to make his home with his sister in Frontenac.

(1941 Obit.)

The Louis Wohlert house on the south side of the Milwaukee Railroad, ca. 1928

Lucille (Wohlert) Eichinger's father, Louis Wohlert, worked for the Chicago, Milwaukee & St. Paul Railroad. They rented a house from the railroad company, which was located across US Highway 61 from the Florence Town Hall, on the corner of US Highway 61 and Ludlow Avenue.

The side track of the railroad was next to the steps of the back outside area. Looking out the bedroom window on the second floor, Lucille could see the train engines, engineers, and the railroad cars as they were idling on the side track.

The house was heated by a hard coal heater (as

Photo from 1928.

railroad cars carried tons of coal to Minnesota) warm by the heater and cold by the outside walls. To get to their outside toilet, they had to cross Ludlow Avenue.

Lucille attended grade school in Frontenac. As there was no bus service at that time to Red Wing, Lucille had to find a ride to Red Wing where she attended and graduated from the Red Wing High School. Several months after she graduated, her family moved to Red Wing.

She married Herbert Eichinger and they moved back to Frontenac and built a house on the corner of County Road 2 and Germania Street.

(Story "Just The Way It Was" told to Evelyn Kiester by Lucille Eichinger and was published in the Friends Of The Florence Town Hall newsletter)

Evelyn Kiester
The Lady in the House by the Side of the Road

(Information taken from interview by Margo Crawford and published in October 2003 in the Friends of the Florence Town Hall newsletter)

As you drive Highway 61, you will see a pretty little house by the side of the road with an enviable view of the lakelette. That house belongs to one of the most active ladies of Frontenac. She is Evelyn Kiester.

Evelyn was born into a family of eight children in Minneola Township, where she went to primary grades in a country school and attended high school in Zumbrota. After school, she worked a short time in Minneapolis, before returning to Red Wing to work at the Stickles Shoe Factory, where children's and women's shoes were made for major markets. It was there that she met her husband-to-be, Lloyd Kiester. They both went to Milwaukee to work in a defense plant during World War II. They were married there in 1943 and would have celebrated a 60th anniversary this spring, had he lived.

While working at the defense plant, they were told that their jobs were ending, as the US was planning to drop the atomic bomb on Japan, so they returned to this area. On their way through Frontenac, they noticed there was a bar for sale. They bought it and called it Cap's Country Club and managed it for five years. It was then that they built their house and Lloyd went into the amusement business and she worked at the Zero King Factory in Lake City, where she stayed until her retirement, having worked there for twenty-three years.

They both became involved in township politics, when there was a rumor that they were planning to turn the gravel pit near their home into a dump. Lloyd was elected to the town board in 1968 and served for eighteen years.

Evelyn lost Lloyd after a five year battle with cancer in 1990. She then went to work granting zoning permits for the township. When the Frontenac Community Center was opened in 1995, she supervised all the bookings for the hall until last year.

She became very instrumental in forming the Friends of the Town Hall after hearing of plans to demolish the historic old building in 1994. She was very involved in getting the building on the National Register of Historic Places in 2000. She is historian for the group and keeps the scrap books up to date.

The Local News

She has been documenting her own family history for twenty years and has also belonged to the Zumbrota Covered Bridge Society since its beginning in 1963, and is very active in that organization, serving as treasurer.

Her love of history inspires a lot of her reading. She collects beautiful plates and dishes with which she has decorated much of her home. She says she loves to crochet and sew material for woven rugs. She liked having garage sales with her sisters and to travel. (Evelyn is now living at Potter Ridge in Red Wing as of 2014)

Edwin Huneke with his team, an ox and blind horse Tom (Photo and article courtesy of the GCHS)

William Johnson was returning home in his "high-powered" motor car, when it became stalled in sand and gravel on a rural highway, and Johnson had to summon for help from a local farmer. The farmer was Mr. Edwin Huneke of Frontenac. "I need help, can you send a team down the road a ways and pull me out?" "Sure" said Huneke, "I'll hitch up right away." He hitched up his team, but what a combination, a well-trained, harnessed-broke bull and Tom, his faithful old blind horse. Old blind Tom, teamed perfectly with the bull and the city motorist was soon out of the rut. Mr. Huneke said he had worked the combination team, successfully in fields, for the past few years.

(1933)

An added part of the story was told by Alice Tackaberry: After Edwin had pulled the motorist out of the ditch, he asked for two dollars for his services. The motorist was appalled at the price, and argued with Edwin. Edwin explained that he had been in the field, trying to finish his field work before it was supposed to rain that evening. It was important for him to get his work done [before the rain], but having to unhitch his team to come to pull the man out of the ditch put him way behind in his field work. Edwin then told him to either give him the two dollars or he would put the motorist's car back into the ditch. (I imagine the motorist paid the two dollars.)

Elevators at Frontenac Station

Alfred Fick, William Savage, and R. A. Paton sitting outside a Frontenac grain elevator. (Photo courtesy of GCHS)

There were two Frontenac grain elevators that were located within the same block between the railroad tracks and Sclavonia Street. One stood behind the Milwaukee depot and the other was located at the west end of the block.

Elevators at Frontenac Station

Frontenac Elevator 1873
(George Dodge)

In December of 1873, George Dodge disposed of his interest in the elevator at Frontenac Station to Mr. Benewitz [Bennewitz].

(1873 Lake City Sentinel

Frontenac Elevator 1874
(Mr. Bennewitz)

G. H. Dodge & Co. Elevator 1880-1882
(George and Dr. R. N. Dodge)

In August 1880, G. H. Dodge & Co., of Frontenac, are building a barley elevator, 28 by 48 feet. They propose to make Frontenac Station a lively grain point this season.

(1880 Lake City Review)

G. H. Dodge sold his elevator to Swetzer & Sauter.

(1882 Lake City Review)

Frontenac Elevator 1882
(Peter Swetzer Sr. and Ben Sauter)

The Peter Swetzer Sr. family lived next door to the Frontenac Cash Store in 1882.

Ben Sauter was in the feed grinding business, and later, in 1923 after Ben's brother, Leo, died, Ben took over Sauter's Garage, and operated it under the name the Frontenac Garage.

Frontenac Elevator 1885, 1891
(McMichael Bros.)

The new elevator of McMichael Bros., of McGregor, Minnesota, is being erected at Frontenac, 32 x 28, capacity 30,000 bushels, office 9 x 24, horse shed 24 x 30 with stable attached.

(August 1885 Lake City Sentinel)

McMichael's new elevator at Frontenac is taking in considerable grain and it runs like a charm. It is considered the best elevator, of its size, from St. Paul to New Orleans.

(1885 Lake City Sentinel)

Frontenac Station grain elevator.

A son of one of its proprietors, is now in charge of the elevator at Frontenac.

(1885 Lake City Sentinel)

Frontenac Elevator
(George Washington Van Dusen)

George Van Dusen, a grain buyer, built many elevators along the railroad line. His elevator at Frontenac Station handled shipments of grain from the area farmers until a larger company bought the elevator, tore it down, and replaced it with coal sheds and lumber yards.

Frontenac Elevator
(The Milwaukee Elevator Company, owners)
(Louis C. Heine, agent 1907, 1913)
(Albert W. Fick, agent 1913-1917)

Arthur P. Taber of the Standard Electric Equipment Co. has just completed the work of installing modern electrical devices at the Milwaukee Elevator Company's elevator in Frontenac. The new system supplants the old gasoline engine. (1917)

Many attractive additions are being made at Frontenac. On this space, where a year ago were the unsightly ruins of old warehouses and dilapidated buildings more ancient than the "Golden Fleece," now stand a well-equipped elevator and lumber and coal sheds, well-filled with a good assortment of material.

(1911 Lake City Graphic-Republican)

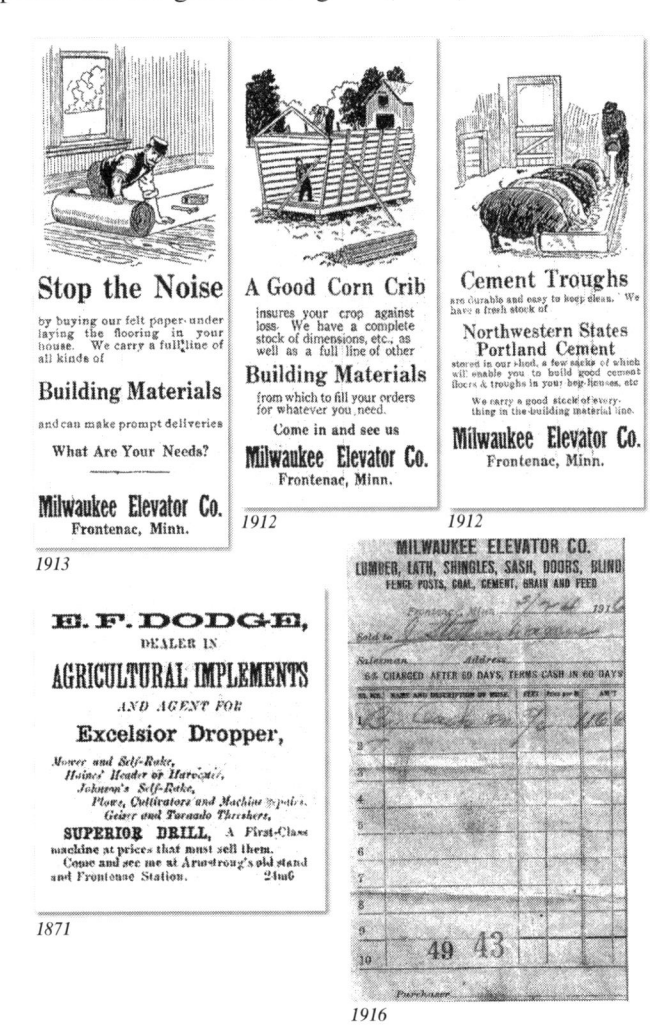

Frontenac Elevator

(Armour Grain Company, owners)
(Alfred Fick, manager 1917-1919)
(Julius Schmidt, manager 1919-1922)
(George E. Newell, manager 1922-1923)
(M. Q. Newell, manager 1924)

The Armour Grain Company had a branch elevator at Frontenac. In 1924 it was under the management of M. Q. Newell, an experienced grain buyer with ten years' experience to his credit, at Harmony, Minnesota, and Frontenac. He has been with the Armour people for seven years.

The investment at Frontenac was $30,000 and a gross business of $50,000. The elevator handles grain, lumber, machinery, fuel, and cement. In 1923 the firm shipped 22 cars of grain.

The Armour Company has some fine buildings at Frontenac, including a grain elevator of 20,000 bushels capacity, coal sheds with a capacity of 200 tons, a machine shed occupying 4,000 square feet and extensive lumber sheds. It has a spur track from the C.M. & St. Paul [Milwaukee Railroad] main line. (1924 Lake City Graphic-Republican)

Julius Schmidt worked at the Frontenac elevator managed by Alfred Fick, who also managed the coal sheds and the lumber yards. After Fick left the company to manage another elevator elsewhere in 1919, Schmidt took over as manager of the elevator. In 1924 the Armour Grain Company sold their elevator, elevator warehouse, lumber sheds, and other buildings to O. E. Zimmerman, but they no longer needed Schmidt's services as manager.

The Frontenac Elevator Destroyed by Fire
(1928 Lake City Graphic-Republican)

On November 19, 1928, the Frontenac Elevator burned down. The Lake City fire department was called, but by the time they arrived, the elevator could not be saved. The lumber shed, a few feet away, was saved and the fire was prevented from reaching the coal shed nearby and the Milwaukee station.

The fire department was handicapped for lack of water but the cisterns that could be reached were emptied. The wind was in the right direction to carry the fire towards the station and across the street, so it was good luck that they got the fire under control.

Mr. Zimmerman, a resident of Lake City and the owner of the elevator, had been grinding feed that afternoon and had left the building sometime earlier. The estimated loss was seven to eight thousand dollars.

Elevators at Frontenac Station

The Frontenac Elevator Destroyed by Fire

(1928 Red Wing Morning Republican*)*

The Frontenac Elevator, one of the old landmarks of the community, was leveled to the ground by fire, and the mill, implement shop and lumber shed, adjoining, were badly damaged.

The Red Wing fire department was called at 5:55 o'clock, but by the time they had arrived, the elevator had been leveled to the ground and the flames were spreading to a large lumber shed nearby. Two cisterns were pumped dry and they were able to save most of the lumber shed. O. E. Zimmerman, who was using one structure as a feed mill, had left the place only a short time before the blaze was discovered.

The elevator, which was situated across the tracks from the Milwaukee depot at Frontenac, was a familiar structure. It was erected some forty years ago and for a period of many years, farmers of the Frontenac community sold their grain there.

Years back, it was operated by the Milwaukee Elevator Co., and later by the Armour Grain Co., which sold the property to Mr. Zimmerman, who operated lumber yards and a coal and implement business along with a feed mill. There was but little grain stored in the structure, although considerable feed, recently ground, was on hand. This and machinery used in running the elevator and in grinding feed and some farm equipment were destroyed. Some of the farm implements were taken out of the store room before the flames had reached that structure.

IN APPRECIATION

Of the splendid work of the Red Wing Fire Department and all those who volunteered and worked faithfully in fighting the fire which destroyed the Elevator, Warehouse and Feed Mill and checked its spread on Monday, Nov. 19, I wish to express my gratitude.

O. E. ZIMMERMAN

Nov. 21, 1928, Frontenac, Minn.

Stone Quarries

Israel Garrard's Stone Quarry
on Garrard's Bluff
(Gen. Israel Garrard, owner/manager 1859-1901)
(George Wood Garrard, owner/manager 1901-)
(William Paton Sr. manager 1907)

The quarry was originally operated by Evert Westervelt in 1853. By 1859 Israel Garrard had taken over the quarry and stone was shipped by steamboat throughout the United States. The quarry was located on what is now State Park land, off County Road 2, between Frontenac Station and Old Frontenac, on a bluff which was called Garrard's Bluff.

Some years ago, Dr. Estes called the attention of the public to a quarry of stone upon Gen. Garrard's land near Frontenac, which he averred at the time was the best building material in this section of the country, being composed of the carbonates of lime and magnesia, and resembling closely the famous Potsdam sandstone of New York.

A sample of this rock was lately shown us by Dr. Estes, who received it from Gen. Garrard a few days since. In color it is a light brown, made up of minute crystals that glitter like mica. It is easy to work and said to be as durable as the earth itself; at all events a building would be grandly beautiful composed of this rock.

(1874 Wabasha Sentinel)

Its light cream stone, used for general ornamental work, was noted throughout the United States, and was used in the interior of the Cathedral of St. John the Divine, the great church of the Episcopal denomination in New York, and one of the handsomest church edifices in America. Among three hundred samples of stone submitted from the best quarries in the world, the Frontenac stone was selected as being the most suited for interior work of the most exquisite nature. The stone from the quarry was very exceptional and was used for the finest and most delicate monuments and buildings.

Soon after arriving from Scotland, William Paton Sr. became a stonecutter at Garrard's quarry, and also a personal friend of Israel Garrard.

After Israel Garrard's death in 1901, his son, George Wood Garrard, took over the quarry business. George took an artistic, as well as a business, interest in the Frontenac product.

By 1907 Paton became foreman and was managing the quarry for George Garrard, who had managed the quarry since 1901, after his father, Israel, died. It is not known when Garrard's quarry finally closed; George Garrard moved his family to Europe in 1907 for his children's educations, but always returned to Frontenac on business at various intervals.

Stone Quarries

Best & Tostevin Stone Quarry 1873-1875
(S. Brown, manager)

A notice in the 1873 Lake City *Sentinel* stated that a St. Paul company opened a quarry in the bluffs near Frontenac Station, with a crew of men under the supervision of Mr. S. Brown.

Recently, a company of architects from St. Paul have leased from E. C. Eaton, who owns a part of this species of rocks, a quarry for ten years, paying twenty-five cents per load for all the rocks taken out. Mr. Eaton informs us that the company are contemplating the building of a steam mill at Frontenac Station for the purpose of sawing this stone.

Best & Tostevin, formerly of St. Paul, wholesale dealers in builders and contractors of stone, have recently established themselves at Frontenac, and are opening up the quarry at that place, and dressing the stone for building purposes. Their work is done by steam power. The members of this firm are both experienced, practical workmen. They have worked in the quarries of Europe and this country, and pronounce the quality of stone at this quarry to be the best they have found anyplace. They don't chip in the dressing as is found to be the case with most stone. They have purchased lots and building houses with a view to make that their permanent residence.

(July 1874 Wabasha County Sentinel)

On March 8, 1875, Best & Tostevin dissolved their partnership, and Tostevin became sole owner of the stone business.

J. F. Tostevin Jr. Stone Quarry 1875-1883

The stone from the quarry was peculiar, being a local deposit of sandstone, hard and very fine when pulverized, and found to be entirely free from dirt, and hardening by exposure to the weather. Above and below this deposit, limestone was found, the sandstone being 12 feet thick. Being fire-proof, it is particularly valuable for building purposes. Tostevin ships the stone to points all through the state and Wisconsin.

Mr. Tostevin, having put up a large mill for sawing, cuts the stone in blocks or slabs to any size, and fills the orders at very reasonable prices. (1875 Lake City Sentinel)

James Francis Tostevin, born in 1845, was the son of James and Sybilla (Smallridge) Tostevin Sr., natives of London, England. In 1847 James Sr. immigrated with his family to the United States, and was engaged in the stone business at Buffalo, New York. Eight years later, the family moved to St. Paul, Minnesota.

James Jr. enlisted in 1862, joining the Western army under Grant and fought at Vicksburg. After the war, James Jr. joined his father in the manufacture of building stone.

Stone Quarries

James Tostevin Jr. was married in 1869 to Henrietta C. Foreman, and they had eight children. In 1872 they moved to Frontenac, where James dealt with cut stone for seven years. While living at Frontenac Station, Tostevin served as justice of the peace. After leaving Frontenac Station, Tostevin continued in the same line of business at Minneapolis and Dresbach, Minnesota.

James F. Tostevin Jr. 1845-1913

1875

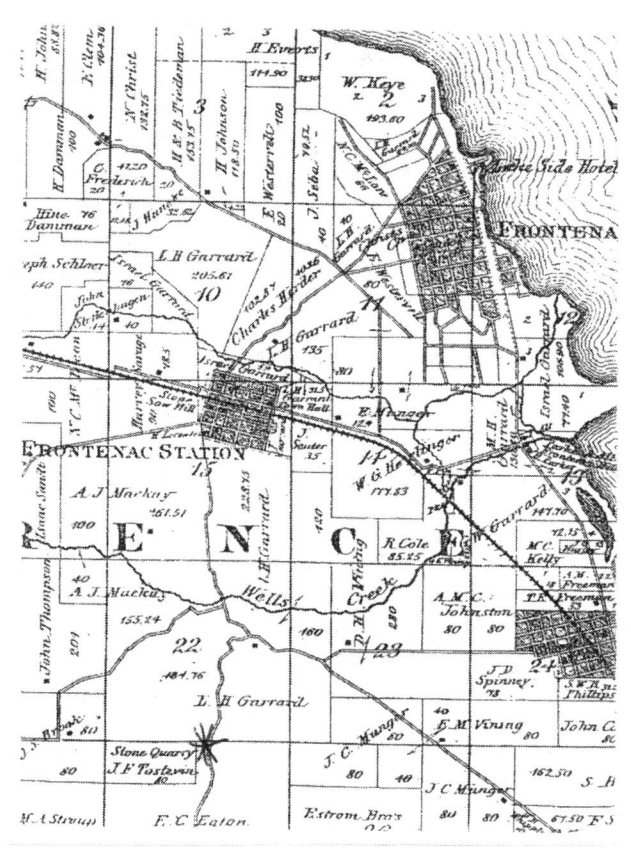

An 1877 map of Florence Township, showing J. F. Tostevin's stone quarry on land leased from E. C. Eaton, south a short distance off County Road 2.

A steam tractor and horse drawn wagon with a load of stone. Photo taken by Albert Keye. (GCHS)

The stone sawmill at Frontenac Station ca. 1874. (GCHS)

The Frontenac Stone Company

J. F. Tostevin Jr. purchased lot 7 in block 6 from Gen. Garrard in 1872 for his residence. Tostevin's house is shown in the distance, on the right of the photo, which is presently the residence of David and Shirley Sommerfield.

Stone Quarries

Frontenac Stone Co. 1874-1875
(Best & Tostevin)

In 1874 Joseph Best and James F. Tostevin Jr. erected a steam sawmill for sawing stone brought from their quarry, leased from E. C. Eaton, off County Road 2. The stone sawmill was located on the right side of Columbia Street (presently US Highway 61), across the railroad tracks near County Road 2, coming into Frontenac Station.

Frontenac Stone Company 1875-1883
(James F. Tostevin Jr.)

On March 8, 1875, James Tostevin Jr. became sole owner of the Frontenac Stone Company whose address for the company was Frontenac or St. Paul.

Mr. Tostevin, having put up a large mill for sawing, cuts the stone in blocks or slabs to any size, and fills the orders at very reasonable prices.

(1875 Lake City Sentinel)

One of the best fronts in St. Paul was built of this sawed stone. Besides building uses, it was used for monumental work, as it took a smooth surface when sawed. Stonecutters in 1880 were Andrew Eaton, George Meyer and William Holcourt.

J. F. Tostevin will furnish $12,000 worth of Frontenac brown stone for a Minneapolis church.

(1880 Lake City Leader)

In 1881 E. E. Steele was the engineer at the Frontenac stone mill.

(1881 Lake City Review)

In 1882 the Frontenac Stone Company had an order for thirty car loads of cut stone.

(1882 Lake City Review)

The Frontenac Stone Co. is making a reputation for the work of their quarry which is rapidly bringing it to the front as the best bed of building stone in the state. Prof. Winchell is on record as having pronounced the Frontenac stone superior to all others in Minnesota, and the company are sparing no pains to put their project upon the market in the very best possible shape.

(1884 Lake City Graphic-Republican)

McIntire and Berglund were dealers for Tostevin's stone and lime in Red Wing, and samples of the stone could be seen at Ole Hegna's grocery store on the corner of Plum and Fifth streets.

Tostevin moved to Frontenac Station in 1872 and stayed for seven years and then moved to St. Paul. In 1889 he moved to West Superior and opened the leading establishment in his line, the firm being Tostevin & Moore, which later became the Superior Cut Stone Company and, in 1896, consolidated with the firm of William Penn & Company. James Francis Tostevin Jr. died in 1913.

Stone Quarries

Frontenac Stone Co. 1883-1886
Lots 5 and 6, Block 14
(Mitchell & Paton, stone contractors)

Mitchell & Paton, stone contractors at Frontenac, have put in a new steam boiler, with other improvements, at the Frontenac stone works and are prepared to furnish all classes of sawed stone, window sill, caps, etc. This stone, has been pronounced by Prof. Winchell, the finest in the state.

(1886 Advance Sun)

The Goodhue County Abstract files have John Mitchell and Andrew Eaton owning this property in 1883, and James Ralston owning the same lots (5 and 6) in 1887.

In the 1885 census, John and Fanny P. Mitchell were living in Frontenac with their children Alexander, Mitchell, Elizabeth, Lucy, James, and Walter. Both John and Fanny were born in Scotland—John on October 25, 1847, and Fanny in 1841. John Mitchell died at the early age of thirty-eight, on January 4, 1886, and is buried at Frontenac.

Frontenac Stone Company 1886-1888
(Lister Bros. stone contractors)

In 1888 brothers James and William Lister left Frontenac and started a stone business, on a small scale, on the Wisconsin side, just below the village of Maiden Rock, called the Maiden Rock Cut Stone Works.

(1889 Lake City Republican)

Unfortunately, their stone sawmill in Wisconsin burned down in 1893.

William Lister married Lena Carlson, December 18, 1881, in Frontenac.

The 1885 census has James Lister born in 1856 and married to Anna Lister with children Walter, Richard, and Arthur and living in Frontenac.

Frontenac Stone Company 1894
(Lister & Mitchell, stone contractors)
(James Lister and Alexander Mitchell)
(George W. Garrard, owner/manager)

Lister & Mitchell, of Maiden Rock and Frontenac, have been awarded the contract for the cut stone to be used in the new Lake City High School building.

(1894 Advance Sun)

Frontenac cut stone is used in the new St. Boniface Church, now being built in Hastings, Mn. (1892) (The St. Boniface Church, in Hastings, Minnesota, was torn down and moved to Bauer's Antique Village, which is located northwest of Miesville. The church has been reconstructed to its original condition.)

Both Red Wing and Frontenac stone will be used in the construction of a stone archway, composed wholly of Minnesota stone, to be erected at the World's exposition.

(1893 Advance Sun)

Alexander Mitchell was the son of John and Fanny Mitchell. John Mitchell was a stone contractor with Paton in the firm of Mitchell & Paton in 1883.

Frontenac Stone Company 1894
(Mitchell Bros. stone contractors)
(Alexander and Walter Mitchell)
(George W. Garrard, owner

All of the building stone was shipped to New York and purchased by the same company that built the Cathedral of St. John the Divine.

In 1895 Andrew Eaton was a stonecutter and in 1900 Christ Larson, John Akeson, and Casper Carsten were also stonecutters, as was Charlie Gohrke who worked many years for the Garrards, sharpening chisels, which were used for cutting and shaping the stones. In 1898 Will Freye and Alfred Frien came from Eau Claire to work at the Frontenac Stone Company.

Mitchell Bros. of Frontenac, have been awarded the contract for the cut stone work on the new administration building at the Rochester Insane Asylum, and also for the cut stone work on the block of L. Mehrkens, on Plum Street in Red Wing, which he will finish this season with brick and stone.

(1894 Advance Sun)

The Frontenac Stone Co., G. W. Garrard manager, is operating the famous quarries at Frontenac and expects to keep a large crew of men at work the entire summer.

(1913 Lake City paper)

Walter and Alexander Mitchell were sons of John and Fanny Mitchell. Walter was born in 1862 and married Amy M. Stone in 1892 in Red Wing. Walter died in 1898 at Frontenac, at the age of thirty-five.

Alexander H. Mitchell was born in Scotland in 1869. He worked as a stone contractor at the Frontenac Stone Company. He died in 1899.

The stone sawmill was located approximately on the corner of County Road 2 and Sclavonia Street.

The stone yard at the Frontenac Stone Co. (GCHS)

Stone Quarries

The Cathedral Church of St. John the Divine

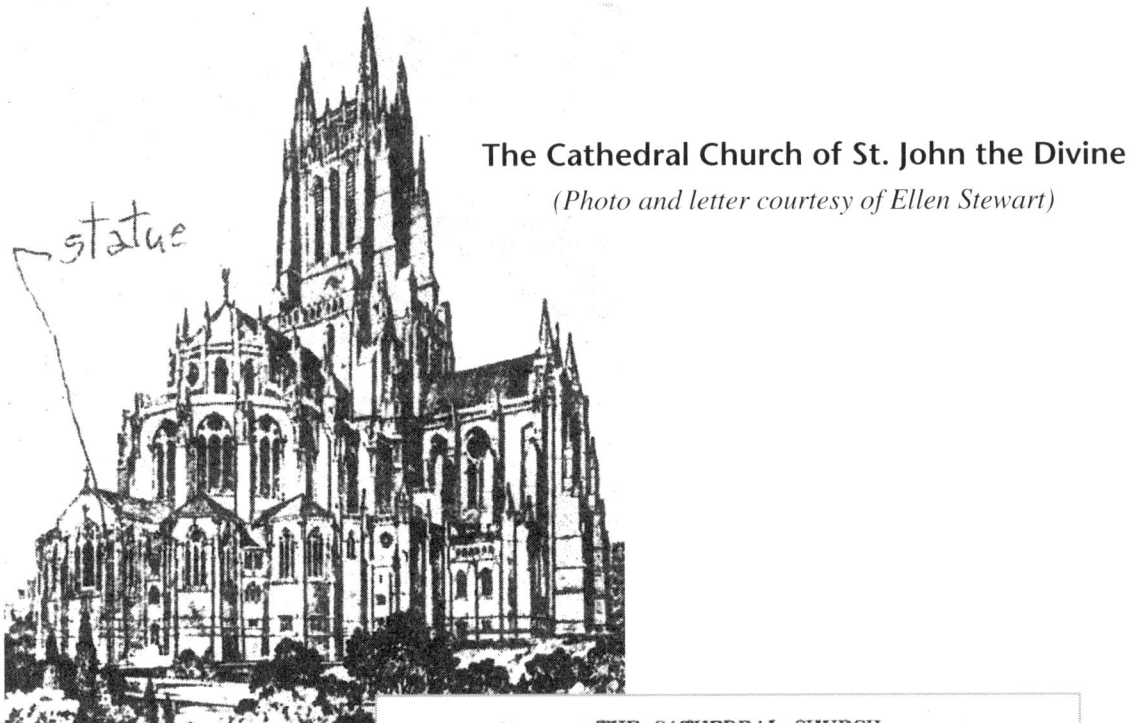

(Photo and letter courtesy of Ellen Stewart)

The East End
The Chapels, Choir, Central Tower
and North Transept

THE CATHEDRAL CHURCH
OF ST. JOHN THE DIVINE
CATHEDRAL HEIGHTS
NEW YORK, NEW YORK 10025

TELEPHONE (212) 865-3600
CABLE ADDRESS "CATHJOHN"

THE REVEREND CANON EDWARD WEST, S.T.D., SUB-DEAN

April 14, 1976

Mr. B.N. Robinson (USAF Ret.)
Rt. #2, Box 232A
Lake City, Minn. 55041

Dear Mr. Robinson:

The statue was done by Gutzon Borglund and it stands in a niche on the north side of the great window of the Chapel of Saint Saviour. You will understand this statue is on the outside of the Cathedral. I have indicated its position on the enclosed zerox copy. The interior facing of the Great Choir is of Frontenac stone. I hope this information is of use.

Thank you for writing.

Sincerely,

Edward N. West

The Reverend Canon Edward N. West
Sub-Dean

Various Mills in Florence Township

The original Frontenac mill built on Wells Creek, in 1856, was owned by General Garrard. It was located near the mouth of the creek near the later site of the Kingsley mill.

Frontenac Milling Co. 1866
(E.H. & Dr. R.N. Murray)

"The Frontenac grist mill which has been in course of erection during the summer and fall is now finished and is prepared to do all kinds of custom work. The mill is situated on Wells Creek, a mile and a half this side of the village on the road from Lake City, is twenty-eight by forty feet on the ground, and three stories in height. The power is sufficient for three run of stone at all times, and the fall being eighteen feet.

Our esteemed townsman E. H. Murray is the architect and proprietor, this being the third mill built by him, in this locality. He is associated with himself, his brother, Dr. R.N. Murray, of Grand Rapids, Michigan, and the company is called the Frontenac Milling Co. In the Spring, they will begin flouring and will ship their flour from Frontenac.

The enterprise and wealth of the proprietors of this beautiful village are being displayed In creating substantial improvements. Mr. Murray informs us that they have begun the construction of a fine avenue from their place toward Lake City, eighty feet wide, which will run along the ridge above the present road. They have the right away as far as Florence and are locating the route, removing trees and obstructions preparatory to establishing a uniform grade in the spring. It will be the finest road in the state, and will afford a good view of the lake. We hope there may be no difficulty in obtaining the right of way the entire distance, although there is some opposition to the road in Florence".

(1866 Lake City Sentinel)

In 1871 the Murray Bros, opened a mercantile business at Frontenac Station

Kingsley Mill

Erastus H. Murray built this mill in 1869 near Frontenac Station, Minnesota which was run by water power. It was discontinued in 1912, by then called the Kingsley Mill. The mill was torn down in 1940.

Kingsley Mill. (GCHS)

Various Mills in Florence Township

Frontenac Mills 1869-1878
(Murray Bros.)

In 1866-67 William Herlinger sold a parcel of land to E. H. Murray (most likely land next to Wells Creek so Murray could build the Frontenac Flouring Mill).

Erastus H. Murray built another grist mill in November 1869, located one half mile east of Frontenac Station on Wells Creek, in Florence township, run by water power and operated by the Murray Bros. Their excellent quality of wheat was patented in June 1873.

"The Murray Bros, are bringing wheat for the Diamond Joe Line from the Frontenac flouring mills."

(Sept. 1870 Lake City Leader)

We acknowledge the receipt of a sack of excellent flour from the Frontenac Mills, owned and conducted by the Murray Bros. At this establishment they use only the best quality of grain for making their flour, and in consequence, it is in great demand. These mills have a reputation for producing good work second to no other in the country.

(May 1871, Lake City Sentinel)

Murray Brothers of the Frontenac Mills have brought us a sample sack of granulated wheat made by their process which was patented last June. Dr. Dio recommended it as a very desirable and healthy substitute for flour.

(January 1874)

Kingsley Mill 1895-1905
(Ammond & Fred R. Kingsley)

In 1891 Lot E. Gaylord sold 2 acres to Ammond and Fred Kingsley on the northwest corner of Frontenac Mill Lot (so called).

The Kingsley Mill, formerly known as the Frontenac Mill, was located one half mile east of Frontenac Station on Wells Creek, and was run by water power. It produced thirty-five barrels of flour in twenty-four hours.

Kingsley Mill 1905-1912
(Fred R. Kingsley)

The mill was discontinued in 1912, and torn down in 1940

(GCHS)

Skinner Mill

In 1870 the Skinner Mill, located on Wells Creek, burned down along with 1,700 bushels of wheat and 100 barrels of flour.

Various Mills in Florence Township

Goodhue County Grist Mills in 1874

N.B. Gaylord Mill   2 run of stone (Wells Creek)
A. Buchholz Mill   2 run of stone (Wells Creek)
Murray Brothers Mill   4 run of stone (Wells Creek)

With the completion of the Chicago, Milwaukee and St. Paul railroad through Frontenac Station, farmers were able to ship their grain to larger mills, including Lake City and Red Wing.

Flour Mills in Goodhue County in 1878

Keye's Union Mill 1878   water, 4 run of stone   (Wells Creek)
George Esby Mill 1878 water, 3 run of stone (Wells Creek)
Gaylord's Mill 1878   water, 2 run of stone   (Wells Creek)
Frontenac Mill 1878 water, 4 run of stone

The Pioneer Press published a list of flouring mills in the State, by counties, giving the location of each mill. Goodhue County ranked third in number of mills and run of stone; being stated at 17 mills and 93 run, but the Pioneer Press makes some omissions in Goodhue County, the correct numbers being 24 mills and 112 run of stone.

F.D. Keye Mill 1871-1874

"F. D. Keye's flouring mill is located about two miles from Frontenac Station on Wells Creek. It was built about 1871 or 1872, at the cost of $25,000. It was considered by everyone to be one of the finest water-power mills in the state. The mill was a four run mill. In 1874 the Keye mill burned down, which was thought to be the work of several tramps who were making this location their headquarters. Mr. Keye plans to rebuild within a few months."

(1874 Lake City Graphic-Republican)

Union Mill 1874-1875

(Kroll & F. D. Keye)

"Vogt & Hill have just finished building a flouring mill on Wells Creek two miles above Frontenac for Kroll & Keye. The building is thirty-six feet square and four stories high; it is built for four runs of stone, but only three are now in. With the machinery it will cost about $16,000. The waterpower has twenty-five feet head."

(1874 Lake City Graphic-Republican)

Kroll and Keye dissolved their partnership the following year with Keye continuing the business.

Various Mills in Florence Township

Union Mill 1875-1878
(F. D. Keye)

"The Union flouring mill a four run mill belonging to F. Keye, situated a mile and a half southwest of Frontenac Station, was destroyed by a fire in July 1878. The loss was $25,000."

(1878 Lake City Graphic-Republican)

"Last Thursday night F. D. Keye's flouring mill, two miles from Frontenac on Wells Creek, was burned down. It is believed it was the work of tramps. The mill had four run of stone, and cost $25,000 four years ago, which with the out buildings, wheat and flour on hand, and the $1,100 in the desk at the time of the fire will make a total of $35,000."

(1878 Red Wing newspaper)

Hoyt & Segar Mill 1879-1880
(formerly F. D. Keye's mill site)

"Dan Crego has the contract for building the foundation of the new grist mill being built on Wells Creek, for $25,000, near Frontenac Station. F. D. Keye has sold his water power property on Wells Creek, near Frontenac, to Hoyt and Segar of St. Paul, to build a large merchant mill. It will be wooden, and cost $8,500".

(Lake City Leader, July 26, 1879)

Hoyt & Segar's flouring mill on Wells Creek, about two miles from Frontenac Station, was destroyed by fire last night. It was considered to be one of the best mills of its size in the state and was built last summer at a cost of $25,000. The fire was caused by the upsetting of a lantern on the top floor when a man was engaged in cleaning something about the machinery. This was the second time the mill was destroyed, having been rebuilt only last fall. Insurance paid $12,000. A mill on the same site, owned by F.D. Keye, was burned about a year ago. Hoyt & Segar decided not to rebuild and moved their families back to St. Paul.

(February 1880 Lake City Sentinel)

At one time, there were four flour mills on Wells Creek; the Gaylord mill at Belvidere, the Esby mill located one-quarter mile east of the intersection of county roads 5 and 2, the Keye mill on the border of section 17 and 20, Florence township, and the Kingsley mill located one-half mile east of Frontenac at the intersection of County 2 and U S Highway 61, at the Villa Maria turnoff.

(info from early settlers and copy from Gerald Burfeind, Belvidere)

Gaylord Mill 1874
(Nelson B. Gaylord)

Nelson B. Gaylord came from Illinois and settled on section 5, Belvidere. He built a small waterwheel in the creek where the current was swift. With this he operated a small mill with which he ground flour for his family and a few neighbors. He called this his coffee mill. He then built a small race and dam, and a building in which to house the flour mill.

The size of the mill was two runs of stone. These were imported from France. It seems the French quarries had just the right quality of flint to make good mill stones. The stones were made in sections and bound together with steel bands. It was about a day's work to sharpen each half.

A 120 pound run of wheat was a good day's grind when there was a good head of water. The mill often had to close down and wait for water. Gaylord had built a thresher in his mill. The first buckwheat that our folk raised, father hauled a load of bundles to Gaylord's mill, had it threshed and then ground into flour.

Buckwheat cakes were a staple article of breakfast food in those days. The buckwheat was set in the evening with a little yeast, and in the morning a little soda was added and then the mixture was baked on a cast iron griddle, and with a generous coating of sorghum syrup added, made a great breakfast.

Gaylord also constructed a sawmill, even though there were few trees in this part of Minnesota at that time, probably a few along the creek and some were hauled from Wisconsin.

(info from early settlers and copy from Gerald Burfiend, Belvidere)

Russell & Son Gristmill 1880-1883

Russell & Son have added a new corn meal bolt to their mill, which is a benefit to farmers to have their meal bolted before it leaves the mill.

(1882 Lake City Review)

The flour mill of Russell & Son burned down in 1883. During its peak operation, it was known to produce thirty-five barrels of flour in 24 hours.

Grist Mill
NEAR FLORENCE.

Farmers beware of the millers who cheat
When you take to the mill a whole sack full of wheat,
For they have all got a unanimous rule
Of taking one-half allowed for toll.

Try us, and see if our rule prove true,
With a respectable grist of a bushel or two.
And when you get home and find you are beat,
Just whistle a tune for the millers who cheat.

BOLTED CORN MEAL
And Graham Flour made on Short notice.

RUSSELL & SON,
Proprietors.

GRIST MILL.

The shades of night were falling fast,
When through the grist mill door there passed
A lad whose dress, to speak precise,
Bore on its folds this strange device.
   Buckwheat flour.

His hat was white, his face beneath,
Was circled with a flowery wreath,
And like a dinner tin-horn rung
The accents of a well known tongue.
   Buckwheat flour.

Across the street he saw the light,
Of cosy fireside gleaming bright,
But only heard the muffled groan
That echoed from the whistling stone.
   Buckwheat flour.

"Another hour," the boss he said,
And then the lad can go to bed,
For in the morning ere you list,
You'll here the cry, "I want my grist!"
   Of Buckwheat flour.

RUSSELL & SON,
Florence, Minn.

Various Mills in Florence Township

Mallan & Gaylord Feed Mill 1885
(formerly Russell & Son)

Mallan & Gaylord will start their feed mill at Frontenac next week. They have purchased the Russell mill site and will erect a new mill in the spring, 30 X 60.

(1885 Lake City Sentinel)

Esby (Esbey) Mill
(R.H. Matthews 1863)
(M. Heschler)
(George Esbey 1878-1886)

The Esby mill was located one-quarter of a mile east of the intersection of county roads 5 and 2. History books say this mill was constructed in 1863 by R. H. Matthews of Lake City, and then sold to M. Heschler, then sold to Esby, then to William Croke.

Wells Creek (Croke) Mill
(Wm. Croke & Bros.   1886-1893)
(A. Knickerbocker   1893-1894)

"William Croke and brothers have bought of George Esbey the custom mill on Wells Creek, four miles from Frontenac Station, and known as the Wells Creek mill, the consideration being $5,000".

(1886 Red Wing Argus)

Wells Creek (Croke) Mill 1894
(Croke Bros.)

"Croke Bros, have resumed running their Wells Creek flour mill, which during the past year, has been leased to A. Knickerbocker. C.L. Harris has been engaged as miller."

(1894 Advance Sun)

Wells Creek Mill
(Frank E. Gronert   1894)
(John Meyer   1905-1910)
(Radke & Radefeldt   1910-1911)
(Henry Meyer)

"Frank E. Gronert has purchased the Croke Mill on Wells Creek and will operate it in the future. Mr. Gronert comes here from Wisconsin, and is an experienced miller."

(1894 Advance Sun)

Various Mills in Florence Township

The mill owners installed turbines as soon as they were available, which increased the horsepower considerably, and the horsepower of the mill probably averaged 25 hp. A bushel of good wheat will mill from 43 to 54 lbs. of flour, according to quality, which would make about 60 one-pound loaves of bread by modern standards.

The owners of the mills started out with stone and later converted to steel as soon as it was available, and put in a steamer to steam the wheat before grinding, making it easier to sift out the bran.

Later, the mill was sold to John Meyer who ground rye flour about 1905 to 1910. The mill was then sold to Radke and Radefeldt who operated it for a year or two, but that was the end of grinding flour and the mill was then used for grinding feed.

Soon the mill was operated by Henry Meyer who sawed lumber by water power. Later, the mill was operated by Mr. Fanslow, then by Ed Scherf who installed a gasoline engine.

That was the end of the former Esby mill—the mill burned down.

(Information passed down from early settlers. Copy from Gerald Burfiend, Belvidere)

Keye and Menzell Mill 1874-1890

The Keye mill was located halfway between Beckmark's corner and Frontenac, and was on the borderline of section 17 and 20, in Florence township. The mill race could be seen from Highway 2 just before one gets to the farm occupied by the Hauschildt brothers.

(Information passed down from early settlers. Copy from Gerald Burfiend, Belvidere)

"The mill stone in the park came from SE 14 of SW J4 Section 17, Florence township. In 1874, permission was granted to Ferdinand Keye and Carl Menzell, to build a mill, with a mill race 4 rods wide and 120 rods long. The right to make a dam, was also granted, providing surrounding land was not flooded. The stone was dug out of the hill near by, and the wagons hauling the stone to the site, where the mill and operators homes were built, were drawn by horse or oxen.

(information found in a hand written letter, written in 1895, by Maud Schmidt, wife of Julius (Jules) Schmidt)

Both the mill and near by home were destroyed by fire, in the early part of 1890.

Blacksmiths

Person unidentified, possibly blacksmith, Nels Carstenson. (Photo courtesy of Florence Township History Center)

Nels Carstenson

Nels Carstenson was born June 24, 1844, in Norway, and settled in Frontenac Station at the age of seventeen. (Information shows that the Carstenson name was sometimes shortened to Carsten). Carstenson was one of the three blacksmiths at Frontenac Station.

In 1878 Israel Garrard sold Nels Carstenson lot 4 in block 14, and it was on this land that Nels started his blacksmith shop near the stone sawmill, near the corner of county road 2 and Sclavonia Street, and what is currently Dan and Carol Davidson's property.

Ellen Holst was born in Sweden in 1862 the daughter of Benjamin and Lena Holst. The Holst family settled in Florence Township, in 1880. That same year, Nels Carstenson and Ellen were married, and by 1895 they had three daughters; Anna, Edna, and Effie. In 1912 Nels and Ellen sold lot 4, in block 14 to Ellen's father, Benjamin Holst.

Nels Carstenson died in 1932, at the age of eighty-eight years old, and Ellen Carstenson died in 1 952 at the age of ninety-one. Both are buried at the Old Frontenac Cemetery.

(William Laidlaw shared a fond memory of playing dominos with Mrs. Carstenson)

Blacksmiths

Gottfried Schenach

Gottfried was a blacksmith in the village of Florence in 1863. His wife's name was Anna (Nannie) and their children were Ariel, Engelbert, and Joseph.

Severin Wegrich 1874

Severin Wegrich [pronounced Wickery] was born in May 1830 in France. By 1857 Wegrich was living in Dayton, Ohio, and his occupation was blacksmith. He married Walburga Ewerz July 20, 1856, in Dayton, Ohio. Their children were Frances, Frank (blacksmith), Dora, Annie, and Regina, all born in Dayton, Ohio. They arrived in Minnesota in 1868 and in 1872 they moved to Frontenac and bought lot 8 in block 2 from Israel Garrard. A blacksmith shop was located on lot 10 in block 2 on Germania Street in 1874. (This leads me to believe that it possibly might have been Severin Wegrich's blacksmith shop.)

Frances married John B. Sauter and Regina married Fred Tomfohr. Severin's wife died in 1883 and Severin died September 20, 1885, and both are buried at Christ Church Cemetery in Frontenac.

Robert Franz 1920-1923

Robert William Franz was born in the Pomerania region of Germany in 1882 and immigrated to the United States in 1905. On May 4, 1910, Franz married Laura D. Holst, daughter of Benjamin and Lena Holst of Hay Creek.

By 1920 Robert, Laura, and their children, Emery, Arnold, Harris, Vernon, Marian, Dorothy, Robert, and Donald, moved to Frontenac Station where Robert Franz purchased lot 4 in block 14. This had been the property of Benjamin Holst, who was Robert Franz's father-in-law. Laura Franz and Ellen Carstenson were sisters, and Benjamin Holst was their father; therefore, Benjamin Holst had two sons-in-law that were blacksmiths.

Franz continued to do blacksmithing at the former Carstenson blacksmith shop until 1923, when Isabelle McKeen purchased the Franz property. The Franz family then moved to Welch, where Robert Franz continued his blacksmithing.

Carl Thompson 1909

Carl Thompson had a blacksmith shop near the Easbey Mill, which was located near the intersection of county roads 2 and 5.

Farmers used oxen to pull the breaking plow through soil which had never been tilled before. Blacksmiths were a very important part of the pioneer community because they made the blades for plows and other necessary metal tools, kept them in repair, and also shod the oxen and the horses.

Early Residents

Michael Ackerman *Barbara Katzenburger Ackerman*

Michael Ackerman
(Marshall and William Laidlaw's great-grandfather)

Michael Ackerman was born in Breslau, Germany, July 12, 1834, the son of Jacob and Annie (Messerschmidt). Michael received his education in Germany before coming to America.

In 1852, at the age of seventeen, he came to America, locating first at Cincinnati, Ohio, where he learned the trade of cabinetmaker. Four years later, he came to Florence Township, settling near Frontenac. For some time, he lived on Wood Avenue in Old Frontenac. He was a carpenter by trade and was employed by Gen. Garrard, with whom he remained for twenty-eight years.

He married Barbara Katzenberger and, by August 1862, he had enlisted in Seventh Minnesota Volunteer Infantry Regiment, Company G, serving in the Union Army during the Civil War, from 1862 to1865.

On January 17, 1870, Barbara Ackerman died of scarlet fever, leaving him with three children: Anna, Edward, and William. William died at the age of ten. His second marriage, in 1870, was to Mrs. Margaret Toppe.

Michael Ackerman was in the grocery business with his son in the firm of Ackerman & Son, from 1885 to 1907, and he also owned eighty acres of land in Florence Township, which he rented out.

His daughter, Anna, married F. R. Trafford on September 3, 1890, and lived in Missoula, Montana. Ackerman split his time equally between his son, Edward, at Frontenac, and his daughter, in Missoula, Montana. He had another son, William, who was deceased at that time. Margaret (Toppe) Ackerman died about 1896 and by 1909 Michael had gone to live with his daughter in Montana, where he died May 15, 1911, at the age of seventy-six. He is buried in Frontenac.

Early Residents

Edward M. Ackerman
(Marshall and William Laidlaw's grandfather)

Edward M. Ackerman was born February 5, 1863. He married Lily A. Menzell, who was born in 1893. They had two daughters, Mrs. Irma Laidlaw and Bernice E. (Bernice Ackerman was living in Minneapolis in 1926.)

From 1885 to 1907, Edward Ackerman was a retail grocer with his father in the firm of Ackerman & Son at The White Store on Columbia Street. Later, in 1915, E. Ackerman was in partnership at the same location with Joe Gercken, in the firm of Ackerman & Gercken, until 1932.

A lifelong resident of Frontenac and well-known pioneer in the vicinity, Edward Ackerman died April 26, 1944, at the age of eighty-one.

Oscar Berlin family

Oscar L. (Bergling) (Berling) Berlin

Oscar Berlin was born in Sweden in December 1854, to Adolph and Gustafa Lind Bergling. The family arrived in the United States in 1866. Later the name changed to Berling, and then to Berlin.

On April 13, 1878, Oscar married Mary Christine Skulstrum and by 1885 Oscar and Mary were living in Red Wing with their children Charlotte, Albert, and Edith E.

Oscar Berlin survived the sinking of the Sea Wing in 1890. Oscar L. Berlin died in 1930.

Early Residents

Joachim and Margaret Damman

Margaret Damman was born in Germany on May 19, 1846. She was united in marriage to Joachim Damman and in 1893 the family came to America and settled in Florence Township. Joachim Damman died in 1910 and, after 1918, Margaret made her home in Lake City.

Margaret died in 1928 and was survived by four daughters: Mrs. Lewis Roper of Frontenac, Mrs. B. Thimijan, Mrs. Margaret Gerken, and Mrs. John Diechman, all of Lake City. Margaret was buried in West Florence.

(1928 Obit.)

Peter Damman

Born in Germany in 1865, Peter Damman came to America when he was nineteen years old, settling in Frontenac, where he lived up to the time of his death. He engaged in farming and converted what had been wilderness into a thriving farm. Peter Damman died in 1944, with one brother, John Damman, surviving him. Peter Damman was one of the early settlers of Florence Township, having made his home in the county for three score years.

Mrs. Peter Damman was born in Germany and came to this country when she was fifteen years of age, and resided at Frontenac for forty-six years. They had two daughters, Mrs. Casper Carstenson and Mrs. E. F. Hunecke. Mrs. Dammann died in 1933.

(1933 obit.)

George H. (Hooper) Dodge 1850-1924

George Hooper Dodge was born in Saco, Maine, in 1850. The family, Benjamin and Elizabeth Dodge, and children, George, Elbridge, and Benwalter, migrated to Minnesota in 1860. They settled in Mt. Pleasant, Wabasha County, where George lived until 1861. That same year, he returned east and remained there until 1865. During this time, his father had purchased a farm near Lake City. When George returned from the East, he attended school in Lake City, where he eventually engaged in teaching.

By the early 1870s, George Dodge had moved to Frontenac Station, and lived in the house next to the Frontenac Cash Store, where he was in partnership with H. Lorentzen. The following year, their partnership dissolved.

Mr. Bennewitz bought the interest in the Frontenac elevator which George Dodge owned in December of 1873.

George Dodge married Harriet Jane Westervelt in October 1875, and went to work for the railroad.

In August of 1880, the firm of G. H. Dodge & Co. (G. H. Dodge and Dr. R. N. Dodge), built a barley elevator, 28 by 48 feet, at Frontenac Station, but sold the elevator to Swetzer & Sauter in March 1882.

Early Residents

George Dodge was also involved in in a dry goods business at Frontenac Station, in the firm of Dodge & Heslin, in 1880, with George's brother, Benwalter (one word), clerking at the store. In 1882 the partnership dissolved.

The firm of G. H. Dodge & Company (George Dodge and his brother, Benwalter) took over the dry goods store, in February 1882, but later that same year, they sold all their stock to Peter Swetzer. Swetzer kept Benwalter on as bookkeeper and assistant.

Earlier, George Dodge had been the station and ticket agent for the Chicago, Milwaukee & St. Paul Railroad at Frontenac Station.

G. H. Dodge moved to Minneapolis, Hennepin County, in 1882, where he worked as a bookkeeper and later went into real estate. George Hooper Dodge died on August 7, 1924.

Andrew Eaton

Andrew Eaton was born in Norway in 1847. Andrew and Ellen Eaton's children were Fred M., George William, and Elsie M. In 1895 Eaton was a stonecutter at the Frontenac Stone Company.

Edwin C. "Aisby" Eaton

Edwin Cirsby Eaton was born in England in 1830. His family immigrated to America in 1851 and settled in Florence Township, where Edwin enlisted in Minnesota Sixth Infantry Regiment, Company C in 1864 and mustered out in 1865 at Fort Snelling.

Rachel (Moore) Eaton was born in New York. Her parents had immigrated to America in 1851 and settled in Florence Township.

Edwin C. (Cirsby) Eaton married Rachael in Florence Township in 1854. Their children were Martha born in 1866, Florence R. born in 1868, Edwin C. Jr. born September 15, 1871, Robert born in 1872, and Hiram born in 1874. It is possible that Rachael died during childbirth after having Hiram, because the following year, Edwin married Julia S. Lucas.

Julia S. (Lucas) Eaton, was born in England in March 1840 and the family immigrated to America in 1856. The family moved to Florence Township and in 1875 Julia married Edwin Eaton. The following year, they had a daughter, Julia B. Eaton.

Edwin Eaton farmed land in section 27, near Frontenac Station on County Road 2, of which eighty acres of the property was leased by J. F. Tostevin for his stone quarry. By 1900 Edwin and Julia S. and their daughter, Julia B., were living in Lake City, Wabasha County. Edwin died September 2, 1909, in Lake City, Minnesota. Julia died November 28, 1928, also in Lake City.

Robert Eaton was born on a farm near Frontenac (Florence Township) in 1872. He was the son of Edwin C. Eaton and Rachel Moore Eaton. He attended a country school near his home and at the age of twenty-one went to Lake City and eventually became president of Gillett and Eaton, Inc.

(1872 Lake City Herald)

E. C. Eaton will sell at auction, at his farm in Florence, March 2, 1892, at 10 o'clock, some horses, cows, and hogs, an unusually complete outfit of farm implements and a lot of household furniture.

(1892 Lake City Sentinel)

Henry Isensee, of Belvidere, in addition to the purchase of the farm of Edwin C. Eaton in Florence, has now purchased the adjoining quarter section of Thomas Gibbs, this giving him altogether 800 acres of land there. This represents a total outlay of about $6,000, and gives Mr. Isensee one of the finest farms in the eastern part of the county.

(1892)

E. C. Eaton was up from Florence Monday afternoon selling some of his celebrated horseradish to the local dealers. Mr. Eaton manufactures a large quantity of this every season, and in addition to supplying Lake City with all that is used there, he has a large quantity which he disposes elsewhere.

(1891 Advance Sun)

E. C. Eaton is exhibiting some fine asparagus this year.

(1891 Advance Sun)

Julia S. Lucus and Edwin Cirsby Eaton

Early Residents

Hiram Eaton and Julia B. Eaton

Robert Eaton, Martha Eaton, and Florence R. Eaton

Early Residents

Abram W. Fountain

Abram Fountain was born in Hamilton County, New York, in 1822. He married Catherine Wheaton in 1844. They came to this county in 1863 and settled in Belvidere Township, where he purchased a farm and resided there until 1877. He then came to Florence Township and purchased eighty acres at forty dollars per acre on section 8.

He was justice of the peace for eight years, assessor, one term, and town clerk for three years at Frontenac Station.

Their children were Betsy A., Melvina M., Ezra B., Jane M., Rosa D., and William P. Two other children, Stephen and Jacob, died. He enlisted in the 148th New York Infantry, Company A, served three years, was taken prisoner at Point of Rocks, Virginia, was exchanged, and died while on his journey home.

Oliver P. Francisco

O. P. Francisco was born in New York about 1830 and came to Lake City in 1856, at the age of twenty-five. He was musically inclined from childhood and at the age of twelve he had learned to play and furnished music for many gatherings.

He was a resident of Lake City and the village of Florence since 1856. In 1870 Mrs. Francisco ran a half-way house on the Red Wing road.

Oliver P. Francisco organized the first orchestra in Goodhue and Wabasha counties. In 1925, at the age of ninety-six, he played his fiddle on WCCO radio, using the same fiddle he had learned to play when he was twelve years old.

(From genealogy of the Albert Keye family)

After the Civil War, he organized another orchestra that was frequently called upon to furnish music for different occasions in Red Wing, Lake City, River Falls, St. Paul, Stillwater, Ellsworth, Mantorville, Pine Island, Mazeppa, and Zumbrota and many other places.

Not only was Mr. Francisco Minnesota's oldest violinist, but oldest old time fiddler and oldest man who ever broadcasted over the radio. He was without a doubt, the state's oldest Odd Fellow, being over ninety-six years old and having belonged to that order for seventy-three years.

(1926 Lake City Graphic-Republican)

Fred Grimm

Fred Grimm was born in Germany in 1852. He married Bertha Sepke in 1878, also born in Germany, in 1852. They immigrated to the United States in 1881 and settled in Florence township where they farmed on Hill Avenue. They had four children: Robert born in Germany in 1880, Richard Jr. born in 1882, Rudolph born in 1885 and Martha (Mattie) born in 1890. Records show them living in Lake Hester, North Dakota before 1910, but apparently moving back to Florence township by 1911. Fred died in 1922 and Bertha died in 1932.

Early Residents

Richard Grimm

Richard H. Grimm married Anna D. Steffenhagen on February 23, 1911, daughter of Herman and Minnie Steffenhagen. They had two children Harold and Arthur. Richard was a church officer and janitor at St. John's Evangelical Lutheran Church for over twenty-five years. Abstract files show Richard living on block 7 and owning lots 4, 10, 11 and 12. Richard Grimm died in 1952 and Anna died in 1979.

John Hager

John N. Hager was born in 1835 in Germany and immigrated to the United States in 1850. He married Ursula Hager in 1866. By 1870 the family was living in Florence township with children; Engelbert P., Margret (Maggie), John F. and Charles N. The 1870 census has John Hager's occupation as a laborer.

In 1870 little John F. Hager drowned while playing and hanging on to an axel of a wagon that was being driven into the lake by a farmer, and the farmer not knowing the child was there.

John Hager owned lot 8 in block 9, in 1872 which was the location of The Frontenac Cash Store. Hager most likely leased the grocery store to H. Lorentzen, in 1878, until 1890.

Hager still owned the property at Frontenac Station in 1880 when he moved his family to Maiden Rock, Wisconsin where he farmed. After Hager's death in 1906, the property was sold to Santelman and Hjermstad.

William Hahn 1834-1921

William (Wilhelm) Hahn immigrated to the United States from Germany in 1855, coming to New Orleans, and working his way up the Mississippi doing farm work until he came to Frontenac. He married Sophia Keye in 1867 and by 1880 was farming in Florence Township on County 2 Boulevard, back by the bluffs. Their children were William Jr., Mary, Emma, Ferdinand, John, Hattie, Lena, and Lottie. The Hahn house burned down in the early 1900s. William Hahn died in 1921 and is buried at the Frontenac Cemetery.

The William and Sophia Hahn house on County Road 2 in Florence Township. (Photo courtesy of Tackaberry family)

Early Residents

William Herlinger    *Nancy Herlinger*

William Gottlieb Herlinger   1822-1903

William Gottlieb Herlinger was born in Northampton County, Pennsylvania, in January, 1822. He married Nancy E. Phillips in 1848, in Pennsylvania, and immigrated to Goodhue County, traveling by oxen and securing their claim of 120 acres at midnight, in 1855. They established their home on Wells Creek near the site of the home of Lulu Monroe, where Herlinger erected a crude cabin and lived there several years.

Mrs. Herlinger wrote home to families in Pennsylvania and New York, telling them that some of the first settlers had to pay $5.00 an acre for land within the Half Breed Tract instead of $1.25

On Nov. 10, 1859, Herlinger was issued 40 acres in Florence township. 112-N, Range 13- W and section 14, according to the U.S. General Land Office records. Eventually, he acquired 176 acres, valued at $40 an acre. In 1870 Herlinger took his corn to Reads Landing to be ground which took three days, round trip by ox team.

The former home of William and Nancy Herlinger and most likely the Steffenhagen house at the time of this photo with possibly August Santelman's three children, Ruth, and twins, Hazel and Helen standing in front. (Photo courtesy of Jeni Stauffer, August Santelman's great granddaughter)

Early Residents

In 1872 William and Nancy Herlinger purchased lots 9 and 10 in block 9 from Israel Garrard. According to a statement made in an article by their daughter, Emma, the first post office in Frontenac Station was located within their house. It was also here, in 1873, that Herlingers added on to their home and opened a boarding house for train men and travelers. Their house was located next to The Frontenac Cash Store which was then being run by Henry Lorentzen and George Dodge.

When Mr. and Mrs. Herlinger celebrated their 50th anniversary, in 1898, some of the guests were; Israel and George Garrard, Herman Scherf, Wm. Mahler and A.D. Kingsley.

By 1905, Nancy Herlinger was a widow and sold the property, lots 9, 10, and 11 in block 9 to John and Frieda Steffenhagen. In 1921 lots 9, 10, and 11 were sold to William Steffenhagen. Steffenhagen owned the property until 1928, when the property went back to Nancy Herlinger. In 1928 Herlinger sold the house and property to William and Grace Wiech which was the beginning of the Frontenac Eat Shop. The house which then had been remodeled into a restaurant was later known as the Frontenac Restaurant run by the "Dutchman", Albert Thomforde.

Herlinger served one term as constable. William Herlinger died March 5, 1903.

Nancy Elizabeth (Phillips) Herlinger 1826-1929

Nancy Elizabeth (Phillips) Herlinger was born in Pennsylvania on December 1, 1826. She married William G. Herlinger in 1848 and in 1855 they came to Minnesota and settled on a farm near Wells Creek. They had four children: Emma born in 1855, Fanny born in 1863, Harry born in 1877, and Orland born in 1885.

Later they had a house built in the village of Frontenac Station, where Nancy Herlinger conducted a wayside inn.

Mrs. Herlinger experienced pioneer life in Minnesota. She came to the territory when it was wilderness, Indians, and wild animals. She knew what it was like to grind flour for bread and to spin, weave, and make homespun cloth into clothes. She was a leader in WRC (Women's Relief Corps) work, and the Lake Pepin Valley Old Settlers Association.

After William died, Mrs. Herlinger moved to Seattle, Washington, to make her home with her daughter, Emma Gove.

An article in 1917 stated that Mrs. Nancy Herlinger, a widow, was at her home in Seattle, Washington, and that she was going to sing "America, My Country" at the reunion of the Department of Alaska and Washington to be held there in a few days.

Mrs. Nancy E. Herlinger, Daughter of the American Revolution and early settler of Frontenac, passed away on January 14, 1929, at the home of her daughter, Mrs. Emma Gove, of Seattle, Washington. She was survived by another daughter, Mrs. C. W. (Fanny) Chandler, also of Seattle. Nancy Elizabeth Herlinger died at the age of 102.

(Obit)

Early Residents

The Hoffman Family

John and Minnie Hoffman's farm was located near Frontenac Station, the first farm on the right on County Road 2. They had three children Albert, Robert, and Harold.

Albert Erwin Hoffman was born May 16, 1905. He lived on the family farm in Florence Township from 1905 to 1930. Albert married Lillian S. Hoffman and moved to a farm outside of Red Wing (Wacouta), well-known for its round barn. Albert died July 13, 1999.

Robert (Bob) married Fern Hoffman and eventually took over the family farm on County Road 2.

Harold married Florence Hoffman and lived on what is now 305th Street where they ran a turkey farm.

The Hoffman Homestead on County Road 2. (Photo courtesy of Ken Hoffman)

The Hoffman Family, John and Minnie with children and spouses: Albert and Lillian, Bob and Fern, and Harold. (Photo courtesy of Ken Hoffman)

Early Residents

The Hoffman Barn. (Photo courtesy of Ken Hoffman)

The sawmill on the Hoffman farm, sawing lumber which built the Hoffman's barn. (Photo courtesy of Ken Hoffman)

Early Residents

Andrew Ferdinand Keye. (Photo courtesy of GCHS)

Andrew Ferdinand Keye 1814-1904

Andrew Ferdinand Keye was born in Brunswick, Germany, in 1814. In 1844 he married Fredricka Uda, who was born in Brunswick, Germany, in 1825. They came to the United States in 1853. He was employed as a stonemason on a suspension bridge at Niagara Falls.

Later they were the first to settle in the Wells Creek area, and farmed sections 17 and 20, for forty years. (The farm was later known as the Norton farm.) Their children were Andrew Henry, Sophie, Elizabeth, Ferdinand, William, Henry F., Augusta, Emma, Frederick D., and Edward.

Andrew's wife died in 1887 and in 1893 he left the farm and moved to Frontenac to live with his daughter, Mrs. William Menzell. Andrew became a citizen in 1896. Andrew Ferdinand Keye died, at the age of ninety, on July 21, 1904, at the home of his daughter, Mrs. William (Elizabeth) Menzell of Frontenac. Rev. J. R. Baumann of the German Lutheran church (St. John's) conducted the service.

(From the genealogy of the Keye [pronounced Ki] family)

Early Residents

Andrew Keye sitting on the right, possibly with friends, Julius Schmidt and Henry Isensee. According to the lumber yards in the background, the location seems to be very near the Sommerfield house, which was supposed to have been a tavern at one time, but their abstract did not show this to be a fact. (Photo courtesy of GCHS)

Andrew Henry Keye 1845-1914

Andrew Henry Keye was born in Hamburg, Germany, on February 10, 1845. He arrived in New York with his parents, Andrew F. and Fredricka, in 1853 and settled at Niagara Falls. Andrew, at the age of eight, got his foot caught in a Ferris wheel and broke his ankle. He was crippled after that, with a club foot.

Still living in New York in 1870, Andrew H. married Dora Maria Wilhelmina Hansen, who was born in 1849, in Wehtenhol, Germany. Three years later, they came west and took up their claim at Wacouta and, after one year, they moved to Wells Creek.

Their children were Louisa Ann, Karl Frederick, who died of tuberculosis at the age of eighteen, Albert Fredrick, Marie Sophie Johanna, and Anna.

(Notes found about the life of the Keye family at Wells Creek)

They lived in a cabin in Wells Creek Valley, which was then known as Thies Valley, where the buffalo roamed. There was a lot of buffalo grass in this valley and the buffalo would gather under the scrub oak and trample the grass. There were few trees in this region. The farmers earned extra money in those days by clamming. The shells were used by button factories in Lake City and Red Wing. In 1893 the Andrew Keye family took up residence in Frontenac. Dora died in 1908 at St. John's Hospital in Red Wing.

As he got on in years, Andrew went to stay with his daughters Louisa Loper and Mrs. E. W. Olson. Andrew Henry Keye died September 12, 1914. The pastor from St. Paul's Church buried him. He was taken to the Frontenac Cemetery in a horse-drawn hearse. His son Albert F. was still residing on the old homestead in Wells Creek.

Early Residents

Albert Fredrick Keye 1880-1966

Albert Fredrick Keye was born May 3, 1880, in Florence Township, to Andrew H. and Dora Wilhelmina Keye. As a young man, Albert worked for the Reichert Bottling Company in Red Wing.

Albert met Josephine Paulina Reide when she was a teacher. They were married in 1903, at the bride's home in Mazeppa. They made their home in Red Wing for one year before Albert bought a farm near Wells Creek. Their children were Harriet Clarissa Marie, Wilhelmina Emma, and Pauline Josephine.

Josephine was chairman of the Florence Township Red Cross. Albert Keye was county commissioner of the Fifth District of Goodhue County from 1937 to 1956, and enjoyed history, gardening, politics, and, especially, photography.

Josephine died in 1945, and the following year, Albert sold the farm and spent his remaining years living at Frontenac Station, across the tracks from the Florence Town Hall on, on Sclavonia Street.

Living in Florence Township for over eighty years, Albert died in 1966 of old age and complications of a broken hip. Surviving him were his three daughters, Harriet Huneke, Wilhelmina Von Helmst, and Pauline Keye.

The Albert Keye family stacking hay (section 20 and 29). The man on the left is Charles (Jeff) Huneke. The man on the right is Albert Keye, and the woman is Albert's wife, Josephine, with the children on the ladder, from top to bottom: Harriet, Pauline, and Wilhelmina. (Photo courtesy of GCHS)

Early Residents

Ammon (Ammund) D. Kingsley 1829-1911

Born in Sardinia, New York in 1831. On March 14, 1857 Ammon Kingsley was appointed U S Postmaster for the town of Lake Land, Wright County, Minnesota. Ammon Kingsley and his first wife, Emarette, were living in Wright County, Minnesota, in 1862. Their two children were Fred and Bertha. On February 8, 1865, Ammon was appointed postmaster for Zellingin, Wright County, Minnesota. On January 13, 1872, he was appointed postmaster for Waverly Mills, Minnesota.

A.D. Kingsley married his second wife, Francis E. Warner on June 15, 1873, in Geneva, Minnesota. Kingsley was in the milling industry at this time.

In 1878 Ammon married his third wife, Matilda A. Phillips at French Lake, Minnesota. Matilda was born in Vermont in November 1843. Matilda had a daughter, Musette, from a previous marriage. In 1879 Ammon and Matilda had a son, Arthur. From 1880 to 1895, the family lived at French Lake where Ammon's occupation was a miller. In 1895 the family relocated to Florence Township and settled near Frontenac village where Ammon and his son, Fred, operated the Kingsley Mill, which was earlier known as the Frontenac Mill.

By 1900, Matilda went to live with her daughter Musette and her son-in-law and family, along with her son Arthur, in Ballard, Washington. Matilda died November 20, 1918.

Meanwhile, Ammon stayed in Florence Township with his two children Fred and Bertha until Fred's marriage to Jennie Weed, in 1905. By 1910, Ammon was living in Hennipen County. Ammon Kingsley died December 8, 1911, in Minneapolis, Minnesota.

Frederick R. Kingsley

Fredrick Kingsley was born June, 1863, in Marysville, Minnesota, the son of Ammon and Emarette Kingsley.

By 1895, Ammon was married to his third wife, Matilda. That same year, the family moved to Frontenac village where Fred and his father operated the Kingsley flour mill.

Fred Kingsley was known to have been a lighthouse keeper for over thirty years at a government built lighthouse, on the point of land where the old fort stood. Every night, Kingsley took his pint bottle of oil and climbed the ladder to fuel, trim, and light the lamp. In those days, the Indians and explorers, in their canoes and keel boats bringing supplies, and new settlers, would see this lighthouse.

(Information mentioned in the history of the Keye family)

Fred married Virginia "Jennie" Weed, in 1905, in Red Wing. Jennie was born October 28, 1867, in Central Point township, the daughter of David and Sarah Weed. After attending schools in the Central Point area, Jennie later taught school there and also at Rush City and Alexandria. Following her teaching career she homesteaded in Minot, North Dakota.

After their marriage in 1905, Fred and Jennie established a home on Kingsley"s Corner, Frontenac. Fred Kingsley's farm was located 1 1/2 miles east of Frontenac on US Highway 3. In 1924 Fred decided to retire from farming, and rented out his farm, and had an auction, where he dispersed all of his farm machinery and livestock.

Early Residents

Frederick R. Kingsley died March 15, 1934, in Wabasha County. Jennie died May 29,1961 while living in Red Wing. They were members of the Christ Episcopal Church, in Frontenac. Both are buried in Frontenac. Fred's sister, Bertha, born in 1865, died in 1914, and is also buried there.

Henry and Frederica Lorentzen

Henry Lorentzen was born 1827, in Hamburg, Germany, and his wife, Frederica, was born about 1825, in Hannover, Germany.

H. Lorentzen was an early resident of Old Frontenac where he was appointed post master August 19, 1864. He also held the position as township clerk from 1865 to 1870. Lorentzen relocated to Frontenac Station and the 1894 plat map shows the land which he owned which was located between the properties of A. H. Keye and Edward Ackerman, on what is now 305th Street. (Presently near Marshall Laidlaw's property).

From 1873 to 1874, Lorentzen was in partnership with George Dodge at a general merchandise store, The Frontenac Cash Store at Frontenac Station, and from 1874-1893, he was sole owner of the business.

Frederica Lorentzen died in 1888 after a long illness. She was among the pioneer residents of the township and county, having resided at Frontenac with her husband since 1855.

(obit.)

The 1895 and 1900 St. Paul, MN. City Directory shows Henry Lorentzen living in South St. Paul with his nephew William Schneider and his family. William, son of Jacob Schneider, ran one of the grocery and provision stores at Frontenac Station from 1878 to 1880. Henry Lorentzen died on June 27, 1901 at South St. Paul, Minnesota.

Since church sermons were spoken in German and Lorentzen was fluent in German, he kindly obliged some of the early residents and gave them lessons in German.

John J. Luth

John Luth was born in 1820 in Prussia. He married Sophia Schwartz, who was born in Mecklenburg, Germany, in 1826. John, at the age of twenty nine, with his wife and son Charles, first sailed on the ship "Annie" and then on the ship "Lizzie", and arrived in New York, NY on May 26, 1854. By 1860 they were farmers living in Florence Township near the town of Florence. Their children were: Charles born in Germany in 1848, John born in New York in 1857, Harvey born in Minnesota in 1859, Lilley, born in 1871, and Mary born in 1879. Sophia died in 1884 and is buried in Belvidere Mills, Goodhue County.

John F. Luth

John Luth was born in 1857, the son of John J. Luth and Sophia (Schwartz) Luth. John married Sophia Miller on May 19, 1881, in Frontenac, Minnesota. Their children were Henry born in 1884 and Caroline (Carrie) born in Wells Creek in 1892. (Caroline married Fred Wiech and they later divorced. In 1939 she married Lawrence Miller). John died October 25, 1916. After John's death, Sophia went to live with her daughter Caroline and Lawrence Miller.

Early Residents

Charles Luth

Charles Luth was born in West Prussia in 1848. He and his parents arrived in the United States in 1854 and settled in Florence Township. Charles married Louisa Schmidt in 1870, who had been born in Michigan in 1851 .Their children were William J. born in 1871, Louis born in 1875, Mary born in 1877, and Martin born in 1885. Abstract files state that Louisa was living on block 4 and owning lots 1 and 6 at Frontenac Station in 1916. Louisa died in 1931 and then William took over ownership of the lots.

The Milton & Isabelle (Hunter) McKeen Family

Milton and Isabelle McKeen with five of their eight children: Myrtle, Grace, Ralph, Roy, and Leslie at their home in Diamond Bluff, Wisconsin, ca. l915 (photo courtesy Lorna (McKeen) Podvin)

Milton Alexander McKeen married Isabell (Isabelle) Hunter, in Pierce County, Wisconsin, in 1883. In 1923 the McKeen family moved to Frontenac Station and purchased lot 4 on block 14 on Sclavonia Street. In 1929 the family moved into the

McKeen's Golden Wedding Anniversary. ca. 1934, Front Row: Milton and Isabell McKeen. Back Row: L to R: Ed Witt, Myrtle Witt, Jack Kent, Grace Kent, Earl Luckman, Roy Mc Keen, Ernie Niedermeyer, Alice McKeen, Leslie McKeen, Ralph McKeen, Roy Niedermeyer, and Mabel Niedermeyer. (photo courtesy Lorna (McKeen) Podvin)

Early Residents

house next to Highway 61 in block 6, lot 8 (former Ed Witt house and later Charley Roper house) with their daughter Myrtle and son-in-law Edward Witt. The McKeen children, Raymond, Ralph, Roy and Leslie also lived at this same residence. Grace McKeen married Jack Kent. Ralph and Roy never married. Leslie married Alice Lorraine Nelson and he worked at the Villa Maria doing odd jobs, lawn care etc. Mabel McKeen married Roy Niedermeyer. Raymond McKeen died in 1930.

By 1935 Ed and Myrtle Witt had moved to Spring Valley, Wisconsin. Milton McKeen died in 1936. Isabell died in 1938 while living with her daughter Myrtle Witt in Spring Valley while Ralph and Roy were still living at Frontenac Station. Edward Witt died in 1945. After his death Myrtle moved to Red Wing with her two brothers, Ralph and Roy.

William Menzel

(Marshall and William Laidlaw's grandfather)

William Menzel was born in Germany, in November 1841. William arrived in the United States in 1851. His wife, Elizabeth, was the daughter of Mr. and Mrs. Andrew Keye. They married in 1868 and had two children, Lily and Mary. William died at the age of eighty-one in 1921.

Elizabeth and William Menzell and granddaughters, Bernice Ackerman and Elizabeth McLaughlin sitting on the lawn near the Menzel home. The house built by Michael Ackerman, great grandfather of William and Marshall Laidlaw, was located on what is now 305th street, and is the current residence of Tim and Sheila Olander. Ca. 1906 (Photo courtesy of William Laidlaw).

Mrs. William (Elizabeth) Menzel

Elizabeth Keye was born in Germany on February 3, 1851 and was the daughter of Mr. and Mrs. Andrew F. Keye, who were among the earliest settlers of Florence. The family immigrated to America in 1851, and lived for two years near Niagara Falls before coming to Goodhue County in 1854. The family homesteaded in a little cabin on the south side of Wells Creek on what they called Keye Avenue Way.

In March 1868, Elizabeth Keye was united in marriage to William Menzel, who preceded her in death in 1921. Elizabeth Menzel died March 6, 1930, in Frontenac at the home of her daughter Mrs. Edward Ackerman.

Mrs. Menzel was survived by two daughters, Lily and Mary, two brothers, Fred and Henry Keye, and two sisters, Mrs. Augusta Everts and Mrs. Emma Gilbertson, both of Argyle, Minnesota. Funeral services were held at the Ackerman home at 11:30 and at St. John's Lutheran Church at 12:00, Rev. Karl A. Nolting officiating.

Early Residents

Isaac G. Munger

Isaac G. Munger, the son of Julius and Annie (Busch) Munger, was born in Michigan in 1834. He came to Minnesota in a covered wagon in 1854 with his parents and located in the town of Florence, at which time he became an agent for various elevators. At the time of his death, he was a grain buyer for G. D. Post of Lake City, and had been township assessor for a number of years. He died in 1893 at the age of fifty-nine, in a tragic accident, being killed by a train. (See article in the "Local News" section.)

(1893 Advance Sun)

Eliab Munger

Eliab Munger had been a resident of this country since 1856, and in company of his father, E. Z. Munger, he came to this state to live, where he succeeded his father in the possession of the old homestead near Frontenac. Unmarried, in failing health, and suffering from Bright's Disease, in 1893 Eliab Munger went to live with his brother, Julius Clark Munger. Mr. Munger was one of the very first settlers in Lake Pepin Valley. He died in 1894.

(Advance Sun)

William Paton Sr. and Fannie (Mitchell) Paton

William Paton Sr. and his wife, Fannie H. (Mitchell) Paton, were both born in Scotland, William in 1863 and Fannie in 1864. They both arrived in the United States in 1880 and married December 31, 1884, in Red Wing. Their children were; Cora, Rachel, Grace, Fannie (named for her mother), Walter, William Roy Jr., and Roy. Between the 1920s and 1930s, William farmed 120 acres between Red Wing and Frontenac.

According to the Red Wing Directory in 1900, William was a stonecutter at Israel Garrard's quarry. Israel Garrard died in 1901 and Paton had the honor of being one of his pallbearers. By 1907 Paton took over managing the stone quarry for George Wood Garrard, as George was busy traveling extensively with his family.

In 1909 George Garrard sold lot 14 in block 3 to Paton and by 1919 Garrard sold Paton the rest of the lots (1-13) in block 3. According to the 1930 census, Paton was then farming in Florence Township.

William Roy Paton Jr. 1894-1958

William Roy Paton was born October 7, 1894, in Florence Township, son of William Paton Sr. and Fannie (Mitchell) Paton. William Jr. married Frieda R. Alpers. From the 1930s to the 1940s, William was a clerk and salesman for one of the Red Wing hardware stores, and by 1948, he was working at Sundberg's Grocery. In the early 1950s, Paton took over Dwight Kinne's grocery store and the name of the store was changed to Paton's Grocery. It was located on the northwest corner of Seventh and Centennial streets in Red Wing. William Roy Paton died March 27, 1958, at the age of ninety-five.

Early Residents

William Frank Paton 1927-2010

William Frank Paton was born in 1927 to William Roy Paton and Frieda (Alpers) Paton. William married Delores Carlstrom in 1948. After the death of his father, Bill, and his mother, Frieda, continued to operate Paton's Grocery. The store closed in December 1965. William Frank Paton died in 2010. (The grocery store was later torn down to make way for a house, built by Habitat for Humanity.)

Joseph and Lena Peters

Joseph Peters was born in Germany in 1848. He and his wife, Lena, who was born in Germany on July 20, 1851, married in 1876. They immigrated to the United States in 1881 and settled in Frontenac Station. Some of their children were born in Germany: Minnie, Anna, and Fritz, while Willie, Louis, and Edward were born in Minnesota.

Carl August Peters, a single person, owned the property next to the Florence Town Hall, lot 7 in block 10, in 1885, Joe Peters acquired the property, in 1889, and also purchased the adjoining property, lot 6 in block 10, in 1920. Joe Peters died in 1923. Lena Peters lived in the home, where she died, for 55 years. Lena died in 1944 and was survived by four children; Mrs. I.D. Hennings of Red Wing and three sons, Fred of Argyle, Edward of Red Wing and William at home. The funeral was at St. John's Lutheran Church with Rev. Karl Nolting officiating. Both are buried in Old Frontenac.

Fred Possehl

Fred Possehl was born in Germany in 1845, as was Fredrika (Fredrica) who was born in 1849. They immigrated to the United States in 1869 and married that same year. After living in Indiana for some time, they moved to Florence Township with their children: Fred H. born in 1871, John born in 1880, Adolph born in 1883 and Minnie born in 1887. Fredrika died in 1906 and by 1910 Fred went to live with his son Fred H. and wife, Frances. Fred Possehl died in 1923.

Fred H. Possehl Jr.

Fred H. Possehl was born September 24, 1871 in Indiana, the son of Fred and Fredrika (Fredrica) Possehl. Fred Possehl Jr. married Frances Margaret Hunecke August 1899, in Frontenac. Their children were Harold F. and George H. In 1911, abstract files show Fred and Frances living in block 2 and owning lot 8, at Frontenac Station. Frances Possehl died in 1916 at the age of 35. By 1919, Fred owned lots 1-5 on the same block.

Fred Possehl married Mrs. Annie Sauter who was also a widow with a son, Raymond. Annie Sauter was born in 1879, the daughter of Johann and Elisa Wiech of Wells Creek. Fred Possehl died November 24, 1931 and Anna (Wiech) Sauter Possehl died in 1956.

Early Residents

Heinrich Christoph August Santelman Sr. 1836-1926

Heinrich Christoph August Santelman Sr. was born in Stederdorf, Hanover, Germany on April 18, 1836, the son of Heinrich Christoph August Santelman and Maria (Meinke) Santelman. He was called "August" most of his life.

August came to America in 1855 and in 1856, arrived in Goodhue County. He married Mary Meinke, daughter of Peter and Maria P. (Wiegersen) Meinke, on October, 1859, in Wells Creek. Maria was born in 1842 in Nottensdorf, Germany. August Sr. worked in Red Wing three years, and then settled in Hay Creek, where he farmed 200 acres, for the next 45 years.

August and Maria had ten children; Mary, Sophia, George Bernard, August Rudolph, William Charles, Benjamin Wesley, Minnie Lydia, Emma Louise, Henry William and Edward.

Edward died in 1923. Their oldest son, Willie, died in 1861. Maria Santelman passed at the age of 62 from the flu in April 1909.

In 1909 Santelman moved to Red Wing to live with his daughter, Mrs. Henry (Minnie) Holst.

August Santelman died in 1926 and was survived by four daughters, Mrs. Mary Braze, Fargo ND; Mrs. Oscar Kruse, Brownton, MN.; Mrs. L. F. Krusse and Mrs. Henry Hoist of Red Wing, and five sons; August Santelman Jr., Frontenac, George and Benjamin of Florence, and Henry and William of Red Wing. August Santelman Sr. is buried at the Hay Creek Cemetery.

August Rudolph Santelman & Mary Wilhamena Steffenhagen

August and Mary Santelman

August (Gus) Santelman and Mary (Steffenhagen) Santelman
1873-1961   1879-1957

August Rudolph Santelman was born in Hay Creek on April 8, 1872, to August Sr. and Maria (Mary) (Meincke) Santelman who were farmers in Hay Creek township. As a young man August was employed at a slaughter house in Red Wing delivering meat to H. L. Hjermstad's grocery store on Main Street. In 1902, after hearing there was a store for sale at Frontenac Station, H. L Hjermstad purchased the store and asked August if he would like to go into partnership with him. August agreed and became manager of the store. That same year, on January 30, 1902, August married Mary Steffenhagen, She was born in Frontenac October 1879, and had lived her entire life in that community. They had three daughters; Ruth, and twins, Helen and Hazel.

(Information taken from a video of Ruth, Helen and Hazel being interviewed "What was it like growing up in Frontenac", submitted by Jennifer Stauffer)

Hazel Santelman was a graduate of Red Wing High School and the University of Minnesota and took her internship at Presbyterian hospital in Chicago. She was employed as a dietician at Lancaster, Pa. hospital. She married Dr. William Stauffer, who was practicing medicine at Allentown, Pa.

(1935 Lake City Graphic-Republican)

Ruth married Henry Hoffert and both are buried in Minneapolis. Helen married Harold Meyer and both are buried in Indianapolis.

Santelman and Hjermstad operated the Frontenac Cash Store from 1902 until Hjermstad's death, in 1931. Santelman then became sole owner and changed the name of the store to Santelman's. In 1943 August and Mary Santelman sold the store to Mr. and Mrs. Sumner A. Rice.

Mary Santelman died in 1957 after a tragic accident where she was burned over her entire body while using a flammable product in the basement of her home. August Rudolph Santelman, known as "Gus" died in Minneapolis, Hennipen County on September 26, 1961. Both are buried at Oakwood Cemetery in Red Wing, Minnesota.

Henry William Santelman 1868-1961

Henry married Ida Mary Kolshorn and they lived in Red Wing. In 1922 Henry was in partnership with his brother-in-law, Henry Holst, in a grocery store on Third Street, known as Santelman & Hoist.

Minnie Lydia Santelman 1875-1971

Minnie Santelman married Henry Holst in 1898 and they lived in Red Wing.

Seated are Emma Louise Santelman and Minnie Lydia Santelman, and standing L to R: brothers, August Rudolph, Henry William, and Benjamin Wesley Santelman. (Photo courtesy of Jeni Stauffer, great granddaughter of August Santelman)

Early Residents

George Santelman Sr. 1880-1944

Born in Hay Creek Township on March 7, 1880, George grew up in that vicinity, and married Elizabeth Steffenhagen on April 3, 1912, in Frontenac. They farmed several years near Fargo, North Dakota, but returned to a farm on Hill Avenue in Florence Township. George Santelman served on the school board in Hay Creek, as well as being justice of the peace in Florence Township for several years.

George Santelman died in 1944 and was survived by his wife, two sons, George Jr. and Marcell of Frontenac, five daughters, Mrs. Harold Grimm, Misses Beulah, Betty, Frances, and Irene of Frontenac, and one granddaughter, Carol Ann Grimm.

Also surviving were three brothers and two sisters: Henry Santelman, Mrs. Henry Holst, and Mrs. Emma Kruse of Red Wing, A. R. Santelman of Frontenac, and Benjamin Santelman of Zumbrota.

George Bernard Santelman 1880-1944 & Elizabeth "Lizzy" (Steffenhagen) Santelman 1885-1953

Benjamin Wesley Santelman 1885-1969

Benjamin Santelman was born in Hay Creek Township on February 14, 1885. He married Frieda Mattia Steffenhagen on September 21, 1910, in Frontenac. Their children included Chester, Kenneth, Rosemarie, and Kathryn. Frieda was born in 1885 and died in 1975. They lived and farmed on Hill Avenue near Frontenac. Ben and Frieda are buried in Frontenac.

Emma Louise Santelman 1871-1961

Emma was married to Lorenzo (Lawrence) Kruse. They lived in Stanton, Minnesota during the first years of their marriage. In 1930 they moved to Red Wing where Lawrence was in a partnership with William Santelman in a South Park grocery store, the firm being Kruse and Santelman. Lawrence Kruse died in 1940.

Benjamin Wesley Santelman 1885-1969 and Frieda (Steffenhagen) Santelman 1885-1975 (Photo courtesy of Barbara Hanson)

Early Residents

John Sr. and Phileppine Sauter

John Sauter was born in Wurttemberg, Germany in 1836. During his first marriage, John and his wife had a set of twins, Joseph and John B. Possibly because of a divorce or death, John immigrated to the United States in 1865. John's second marriage was to Phileppine Sauter who was born in Germany on August 6, 1842 and immigrated to America in 1858. The 1865 census has John and Phileppine living in Hay Creek. By 1870, they were living and farming in Florence township. The 1873 abstract files show John owning lots 5, 12, and 13 in block 8 at Frontenac Station. John was also a grain dealer in Frontenac. They had ten children: Flora, Albert, Augusta, August, Rosa, Frank, George, Francis, Isabel, and Leonora. In 1888, the family moved to St. Paul, MN.

"John Sauter, who until eight or ten years ago, was a grain dealer at Frontenac, died at his home, 465 Park Avenue, St. Paul, yesterday, at the age of 61 years. The funeral takes place Friday. The deceased leaves a family in St. Paul and relatives in Florence."

(1895 obit. Daily Republican)

In 1920, Phileppine was living with her daughter, Flora, and her family, in St. Paul. Phileppine died in St. Paul on February 9, 1920. Both John and Phileppine are buried at Calvary Cemetery in St. Paul.

Augustine Sauter and Agathe (Schafer) Sauter

Augustine (August) Sauter was born October 19, 1854, in Wurttemberg, Germany. Augustine was a brother to John Sauter Sr. August married Agathe (Agatha) Schafer who was born June 17, 1853. Their children were; Mary, Ferdinand (Fred), Leo, Frank and Bernhart (Ben). By 1870, August and Agathe were living in Florence township and farming on 120 acres near Frontenac Station. By 1888, August and his family were living on lot 5 in block 9. Agathe died March 13, 1892. After Agathe died, August went to live with his son, Ben, and his wife, Henrietta. Augustine died November 16, 1915. Both are buried at the Calvary Cemetery in Red Wing.

Bernhardt (Ben) and Henrietta Sauter

Ben Sauter was born on November 17, 1884 to Augustine and Agatha (Schafer) Sauter. He married Henrietta and they had one daughter, Isabelle. Ben Sauter did general farming before entering into the garage business. In 1923, after his brother, Leo, died Ben took over Leo's garage, known as Sauter's Garage and renamed the garage, The Frontenac Garage.

Bernhart Sauter died March 1978, at the age of 92 and is buried at Frontenac.

Ferdinand (Fred) Sauter

Ferdinand Sauter has purchased the John Fredericks farm on which Fred Possehl has been a tenant for several years.

(1911 Lake City Graphic)

Early Residents

The house on the right was the home of Leo and Anna (Wiech) Sauter in 1916 and is presently the home of Mrs. Arland Adler. Both houses still stand on Sclavonia Street. (GCHS)

Leo Sauter

Leo William Sauter was born October 3, 1879, to parents, Augustine and Agatha (Schafer) Sauter, who farmed near Frontenac. Leo married Anna Wiech on November 14, 1906, in Red Wing. They had one son, Raymond. Between 1907 and 1909 Leo was a barkeeper in Red Wing. In 1909 he moved his family to Lake City where he operated the Lakeview Hotel until 1911 when he returned to Frontenac Station.

Between 1915 and 1918 Sauter purchased lots 7, 8, 9, 10, and 11 in block 11 on Sclavonia Street.

In 1920 Leo and Anna Sauter purchased lots 5, 6, and 7 in block 9, from August and Mary Santelman. That same year Leo built a confectionery store on the southern part of lot 7. In 1921 Leo built a service garage, on the northwest corner of Scandinavia and Germania streets (presently the parking lot for B. Wells bar). In 1922 Leo sold his confectionery store to Edward and Louis Peters which they remodeled for a billiards and bar business. Peters Bros. Billiards was located on Scandinavia Street, next to Sauter's Garage and behind August Santelman's grocery store.

In 1923 Leo and Anna Sauter bought lot 2 in block 11 on Sclavonia Street, from Albert and Bertha Schmidt. That same year they purchased lots 1 and 2 in block 12. These lots were owned by the Sauter family until 1949, when they were sold to Virgil and Violet Martinson.

(Info from Goodhue County Abstract files)

Soon after Leo and Anna Sauter purchased Albert Schmidt's tavern early in 1923, Leo died at the age of forty-two at the end of March. He was survived by his wife, Anna, son Raymond, a sister, Mrs. John Damman of Wacouta, and two brothers, Frank of Hopkins and Ben of Frontenac. His funeral was held at the Villa Maria where Rev. Oliver Dolphin, of St. Joseph's Church of Red Wing, officiated.

(1923 Obit.)

Early Residents

John B. Sauter Jr. and Frances (Wegrich) Sauter

John B. Sauter was born March 19, 1856 in Wurttemberg, Germany along with his twin brother, Joseph. They were sons of John Sr. and his first wife. There was possibly a divorce or death of a parent and in 1865, John Sr. left Germany and arrived in America.

John Jr. and his twin brother, Joseph, left Germany on the ship, Allemannia and arrived in America, in 1872. In 1878, John B. married Frances Wegrich in Red Wing. John was Superintendent of schools. By 1880, John, Frances and their two daughters, Mary and Elizabeth were farmers in Florence township. Frances Sauter died in 1887. By 1910, John, a widower, was working as a hired hand at the Villa Maria. John Sauter died April 22, 1913 in an accidental drowning in Lake Pepin. Both he and Frances are buried at Calvary Cemetery in Red Wing.

Joseph William Sauter

Joseph Sauter and his brother John B. were twins (born one day apart). They were born in Wurtemburg, Germany on March 19, 1856 to John Sauter Sr. and his first wife. Joseph and John B. arrived in the United States in May of 1872. Their father, John Sauter, was already in the United States with his second wife, Phileppine and family.

The 1880 census has Joseph living in Florence township and farming on the other side of Wells Creek. Joseph married Maria (Mary) Caroline Huneke, June 6, 1882. The 1894 plat map has Joseph still farming there. By 1900, the family was living in Goodhue. Later, Joseph and Mary relocated to Stevens County, near Morris, MN where Joseph and his sons ran a corn shelling business. Joseph died in 1930.

Harvey and Mariette Savage

Harvey Savage was born in New York state, in 1824 the son of John Savage and Hannah (Skinner) Savage. On May 2, 1852, at the age of 27, Harvey married seventeen year old, Marriette (Maryette) Sherman, at Marcellus, Michigan. Marriette was also born in New York, in 1835. In 1854 they came by railroad to Galena, Illinois, and then by boat to Frontenac, Minnesota. They built a log cabin on the present Savage farm, which is located near Frontenac Station, under the oak trees in the east field. They had five trees named for themselves and their three sons. The three sons were; Lewis H., Charles I., and William. Marriette Savage died in 1914 and Harvey Savage died in 1919, at the age of 95. Both are buried in the Old Frontenac Cemetery.

Harvey & Marriette (Maryette) (Sherman) Savage

(1919 obit.)

Early Residents

Lewis Harvey and Flora Savage

Louis Harvey Savage was born at Frontenac on April 24, 1885, son of Harvey and Marriette Savage. At the age of 29, he married Florence (Flora) Steffenhagen, in 1914. Louis farmed in Florence township. They had five children; Laura, Mrs. Louis Thimijan, (Wells Creek), Lucy, Mary, Charles and John L. (died 1970). Louis died June 1, 1936 at the age of 81. Florence died March 20, 1947 at the age of 84.

(1936 obit.)

Louis (Lewis) Harvey & Flora Savage

Charles Irving and Emma Savage

Charles Irving Savage was born November 18, 1860, the son of Harvey and Mariette Savage. On May 31, 1887, he married Emma Mortenson in Red Wing. Later they moved to Oregon. In July 1898 the family came back to Frontenac with the intention of making their future home at his father's home and taking charge of the farm. They had a son Charles Jr. born March 10, 1929, in Florence Township. (Charles Jr. died September 2011). By 1930 they were living in Brownsville, Oregon. They had another son Donald Eugene who was born May 24, 1931. (Donald died August 12, 2011). Charles I. died in July 1940 at Brownsville, Oregon, at the age of seventy-nine.

William Henry and Nettie Savage

William Henry Savage was the third son of Harvey and Mariette Savage and came with his parents to this county from Michigan in 1854, homesteading the farm which has since been the home of the family. William was born in Frontenac on June 22, 1864. He was educated in the local schools and attended Carleton College at Northfield for one year. He graduated from Cornell College in Mount Vernon, Iowa, in 1886, specializing in civil engineering. He taught in public schools for a few years, and then followed his chosen work, surveying, in the states of Washington, Idaho, and Montana for ten years.

Returning to Frontenac, he married Nettie Savage on June 1, 1915. They had no children. William farmed for a few years before leasing The White Store from E. M. Ackerman. He conducted the general store from 1907 to 1915. During this time he filled several public offices, including town treasurer and school board clerk.

In 1929 William had an auction and rented out the Savage farm. By 1930 William was divorced and boarding at the house of Fred R. and Jennie Kingsley.

He was a member of the Christ Episcopal Church in Old Frontenac. W. H. Savage died December 12, 1935. He was survived by two brothers, L. H. Savage of Frontenac and Charles Savage of Roseburg, Oregon. Three nieces, Mrs. Guy Dunham of Oak Center, Mrs. Louis Thimijan of Frontenac, and Mrs. Whitney of Roseburg, Oregon, and four nephews, Charles and John of Frontenac, Sherman and Harvey of Roseburg, Oregon.

(Information from obituaries and the Charles Savage family)

Early Residents

Charles Harvey Savage

Charles H. Savage was born February 28, 1895, to Lewis and Flora Savage. He married Blanche Lloyd Brock, who was born in 1899. Their children were William, Ruth Ann, June, Philip, Marjorie, C. Vernon, Mary Jean, Donald, Evelyn, Janette, Jack, and Shirley. Blanche died in 1946 and Charles Harvey Savage died October 13, 1983.

The Family of
Engelbert (John) Schenach and
Maria Sophia Henrietta (Friedrichs) Schenach

Engelbert (John) Schenach 1832-1922

John Schenach, the son of one of the German families Gen. Garrard brought to the area, was born in the Tyrolean area of Germany in 1832. In 1861 he married Maria Sophia Henrietta Friedrichs, who was born in 1838 and immigrated to the United States in 1859. In 1870 they were living on a farm of 150 acres a short distance from Frontenac Station with their children Clara, Louis, E. M. (Edmund), Frank, Bertha, Fredrick, Emily, Emma (who was a school teacher), and Francis.

John was the leader of the Frontenac Band. His cornet is on display at the Goodhue County History Center. He was one of Israel Garrard's pallbearers.

Maria died in 1913 and John died April 15, 1922, at the age of ninety, and they are both buried in Old Frontenac.

Bertha (Schenach) Schmidt

Bertha married Albert Schmidt. (See the story of Albert Schmidt.)

Louis G. Schenach 1863-1936

Louis Schenach, son of Engelbert and Maria Schenach, was never married and farmed on his parents farm. His sister Emma, also single, was a school teacher at school district 24 in 1907, and also lived on her parents farm. Later, Emma lived with her brother, Louis, on the farm.

Edmund Martin (E. M.) Schenach 1865-1962

E. M. Schenach was born in 1865 in Frontenac. He married Mary A. Taggert, born in 1862, and their children were Raymond, Ruth, Harold, Bernard, and R. Lawrence. They lived in Florence Township from 1865 to 1895. For some years he was employed at the Red Wing Marble Works of J. F. Oliva. In 1891 Ed and his brother Frank, who also lived in Frontenac, purchased the marble works of U. Shebat at Wabasha. By 1894 Ed and Mary Schenach had moved to Red Wing, where Ed was a partner with J. M. Vickers in the National Marble & Granite Works on Main Street. From 1903 until 1910 E. Schenach had a marble business at 318 Fourth Street. Later, in 1946, he ran the business Monuments and Markers at 213 Plum Street. Mary died in 1947 and Edmund died in 1962. Both are buried in Frontenac.

Frank Schenach 1868-1931

Frank Schenach was born May 3, 1868, in Frontenac. In 1890 he moved to Red Wing and learned the marble cutting trade. He married Julia T. Quigley on November 14, 1894. Their children were Mary, Leo, and Frances.

After three years (in 1893), they moved to Wabasha where he opened a marble works, which he operated until 1898. That same year they moved back to Red Wing. He continued in the marble business until 1905. Schenach became a rural mail carrier for Red Wing, continuing in this occupation for eleven years. Later he was employed as a mechanic at the Red Wing Motor Company. Frank J. Schenach died July 1, 1931.

Emmanuel Schenach 1835-

Emmanuel Schenach was born in Germany in April 1835. He immigrated to the United States in 1862 and arrived in Florence Township in 1863. His occupation was wagonmaker in the town of Florence, in 1870. His wife was Anestasia (Anna) and their children Jose, Victoria, Dora, and John. Later they had a farm in section 5.

Gottfried Schenach

Gottfried Schenach was born in Tyrol, Germany in 1825. His wife Annie was also born in Tyrol in 1834, as was their first child, Ariel. By 1863, they were living in the town of Florence where Gottfried's occupation was listed as blacksmith. Later, Engelbert and Joseph were born in Florence Township.

Herman Scherf

Herman Scherf was born in 1842 in Germany and immigrated to the United States with his parents, in 1848. He married Caroline Steffenhagen in 1869, who was born in Germany in 1853 and immigrated to the United States with her parents, in 1863. Herman and Caroline's children were; Emily, William, Nettie, Harry and Etta. On April 15, 1893, Herman was appointed postmaster at Frontenac Station, a position he held until 1915. After Herman's death, in 1918 Caroline moved to Red Wing where she died in 1927. Herman and Caroline are buried in the Frontenac Episcopal Cemetery.

Harry Herman Scherf

Harry Herman Scherf was born in Frontenac on July 6, 1888, the son of Herman and Caroline Scherf. He spent all but twenty years in that community. He spent eighteen years as machinist for the Red Wing Motor Company.

Harry Herman Scherf died in 1944. His wife, Clara, predeceased him. Survivors included his daughter, one brother, William Scherf, of Red Wing, three sisters, Mrs. L. C. Tackaberry and Mrs. Carrie Carlson of Frontenac (an innkeeper in 1940), and Mrs. H. J. Boatman.

Albert and Bertha (Schenach) Schmidt

Albert Schmidt was born in Frontenac on December 17, 1860, the son of Charles and Maria Schmidt from Mecklenburg, Germany. After coming to America his parents settled in Wabasha County, where they farmed.

Bertha Schenach was born in Frontenac October 13, 1871, in a house on the site where the Co-operative Creamery was later built.

On June 20, 1894, Albert married Bertha Schenach of Frontenac. That same year he was in partnership with C. F. J. Haustein, running a general merchandise store called Haustein & Schmidt on Sclavonia Street. The following year the partnership was dissolved and Albert went into the tavern business.

Albert and his family lived in the rear and upstairs of the saloon until 1908 when they acquired lots 9 and 10 in block 8 near The White Store. (That house still stands today.) In 1916 George Garrard sold lot 7 and 8 in block 8 to Albert Schmidt.

In 1920 Schmidt was managing the shipping for the Frontenac Co-operative Association.

In 1923 Albert and Bertha sold the tavern to Leo and Anna Sauter and in 1924 Albert became vice president of the Frontenac State Bank.

Albert's activities had slowed down over the years, due to a previous automobile accident. Swerving to avoid hitting a dog in the road, he hit a small road drag and the car went over the bank.

Albert Schmidt died of a heart attack on December 16, 1934. He was survived by his wife, Bertha, and four children: Mrs. J. S. (Betty) Schmidt, Frontenac; Mrs. D. Tackaberry, Hollywood, California; Miss Minnie Schmidt, at home; and Howard, and a brother, Ed Schmidt of Spokane, Washington.

Early Residents

The former Albert Schmidt house on US Highway 61 next to The Whistle Stop. John Schmidt lived in this house in 1907 and Albert and family lived there in 1908. (Photos taken in 1980, courtesy of Judy Steffenhagen.)

The Schmidt Family

Most of the information on the Schmidt family came from a thirteen-page letter handwritten by Maud Schmidt. In this letter Maud explains, in her own words, the story of the Schmidt family. This valuable piece of history on the Schmidt family was graciously submitted by Laura Stemper for this book.

Charles and Maria (Lange) Schmidt

Charles and Maria Schmidt were married in Mecklenburg, Germany. Maria's parents were Wilhelm and Anna (Kitzrows) Lange. Charles was called Carl. (This is the German form of the name.) They stayed at Columbus, Wisconsin, with relatives on their arrival to the States. There were more relatives living in Lake City and surrounding areas.

It was a struggle to get started farming in Wabasha County, as there were few pieces of machinery available at that time. Maria's parents, Wilhelm and Anna, lived with them on the farm, as did Anna's parents.

Charles and Maria had five children: Bertha, Pauline, Josephine, Julius (Jule), and Albert. The family always called Julius "Jule." The farm boys seldom could attend school regularly in the spring and fall, as there were too many chores that had to be done.

The girls, Bertha and Josephine, married near their twentieth birthdays. Bertha had married a Lange, who had a furniture store in Lake City and, a few years later, Josephine married William Jacobs, who was a cattle buyer. Pauline died while in her early twenties.

Early Residents

The Story of Julius (Jule) Schmidt
(son of Charles and Maria Schmidt)

Eventually Charles and Maria Schmidt and Jule left the farm and moved to Lake City, where Jule found a job working for Mr. Grannis, who owned a paint store.

During this same time, Al Fick was the manager of the elevator in Frontenac. Since the company was expanding, adding coal sheds, and needing another man, Fick asked Jule if he would come to Frontenac and work for him at the elevator, and Jule did.

It was at August Santelman's grocery store that Jule met Maud Schenach in 1916. Cora Paton introduced them, and, on August 11, 1918, Julius and Maud were married. Her sister Alberta was the bridesmaid and Leo Schenach was the groomsman. (By this time, Jule's father had died.) Albert and his wife Clare did not come as Clare was pregnant and women at this time did not often go out in public when they were pregnant. After the honeymoon Jule rented the downstairs of Mrs. Damman's house.

Jule worked at the elevator, as there were also coal sheds and a lumber yard to manage. There had been another grain elevator nearby, but it was torn down and replaced with coal sheds when a larger company bought the elevator.

The farmers from Goodhue, Bellechester, and the surrounding area hauled grain to Frontenac Station. The grain was then shipped out in boxcars to various parts of the United States.

Later Al Fick was offered a better paying job, managing an elevator in another town, which opened up the manager position at the Frontenac elevator for Jule. The elevator was sold in 1922, and Jule wasn't needed, so he had to look for another job.

Jule bought and managed a pool hall in Waverly, Minnesota. At that time, hard liquor, sold under the counter, was expected. Not wanting to get caught in this position, Jule sold the business and they moved to Red Wing. Jule got a job working for B. A. Olson, a well-known paint store owner. They lived in Red Wing from the fall of 1923 to October 1926.

Ben and Henrietta Sauter rented Schmidt's house in Frontenac for three years, when they decided to build a house of their own.

Jule and Maud (or Maude) had four children: Lorraine (Mrs. Erick) Mueller, Frederick, Mary, and Donald. In October that same year they moved back to Frontenac Station into their old house vacated by the Sauters. Jule still worked for B. A. Olson in Red Wing and also did woodcutting and miscellaneous jobs to make ends meet. Bertha Lange, Jule's sister (everyone called her Aunt Bert) came to stay quite often.

In 1939 Julius purchased The White Store at Frontenac Station from Emil Wohlers. In 1946 Julius sold the business to Rudy and Maxine Charlson and he retired. Julius Frederick Schmidt died that same year.

Maud Schmidt got into township government in 1946 when she finished the unexpired term of her late husband. She continued acting as township treasurer for the next twenty years.

Early Residents

Maude Henrietta Schmidt
(daughter of Albert and Bertha (Schenach) Schmidt)

Maude Henrietta Schmidt was born November 5, 1895, in Frontenac. Her parents were Albert and Bertha (Schenach) Schmidt, who were both born in Minnesota. Bertha was born on October 13, 1871, in a house on the site where the creamery was built years later.

Bertha married Albert Schmidt on June 20, 1894. Albert and Bertha's first home was built as an extension of a saloon located on Sclavonia Street. There were three rooms downstairs and two rooms upstairs. There was a large room between the saloon and their living room, where women could sit. Twice a year Albert would cook squirrel, rabbit, or venison and serve it to his customers.

Maud Schmidt - Florence Township Board Member Treasurer

(This tavern building was moved from Old Frontenac approximately in 1879 to Sclavonia Street and was always occupied as a tavern, until it burned down in 1939.)

Maud's brother, Clarence, was born August 12, 1898, but died in March of 1899. Emily also died. Alberta was born later, as were Howard and Lucille.

Maud started school the fall after her seventh birthday and later went to Red Wing High School. She boarded with her Uncle Frank and Aunt Julia during high school. She studied and became a teacher. Maud taught school in 1914 and 1915 for two terms. The first two years of teaching were in a school seven miles from her home. The following school term, she taught at the Wells Creek School, which was on Uncle Julius's farm. Her mother, Bertha Schenach, and her Aunt Em also taught at country schools.

In 1917 Maud had a chance to go to Spokane, Washington, with Uncle Edward and Aunt Frances Schmidt. She went by train to Tacoma and stayed with her Uncle John and Aunt Clara Kade. She got a job clerking in a department store and later had a job in a furniture factory.

In September of that year, the Goodhue County schools called Maud's mother and asked if Maud could teach school near Goodhue. Maude came back to Minnesota in October 1917 and took the teaching job. After Maud's return to Minnesota, Jule bought her a ring in February and they were married in August 1918.

Early Residents

Julius Schmidt Sr.

Julius Schmidt Sr. was born February 25, 1865. Julius and his wife, Henrietta, were both born in Bavaria. By 1875 they had six children: Doris, Frances, Minnie, Albert, Julius, and Edward. Julius was a farmer. Julius Schmidt Sr. died October 19, 1929.

Jacob Schneider

Jacob Schneider was born in Hesse-Darmstadt, Germany, on November 24, 1831. He immigrated to America in 1851 and lived for a year in New York. In 1856 he married Dorothea Shale, who was also born in Germany. They came to Florence Township in 1858 and settled in Old Frontenac. In 1861 he enlisted in the infantry and served three years. In 1865 Schneider returned to Frontenac and opened a tavern. He resided there until 1872 when he bought some land at Frontenac Station from Israel Garrard. That same year he opened a grocery and provisions store.

Jacob's wife, Dorothea, died on March 18, 1887 and is buried in the Frontenac Cemetery. That same year, on December 22, 1887, Jacob and Barbara Schneider married.

Jacob Schneider died on April 29, 1893, and is also buried in the Frontenac Cemetery.

Mr. Jacob Schneider, an old and respected resident of Frontenac, died of heart failure at the age of 61. He was buried from the German Lutheran Church in Frontenac, Rev. Chr. Bender officiating. The funeral services were very largely attended.

(1893 Advance Sun)

William Schneider

William Schneider, son of Jacob and Dorothy Shale Schneider, was born in Cincinnati, Ohio in 1852 or 1853 (dates vary). He and his parents arrived in Goodhue County and Frontenac village in 1862. (The History of Goodhue County states 1858). As a young man, William worked at his father's grocery and provisions store on Sclavonia Street. In 1875 William married Charlotte Fraund, who was born in Germany in 1854 or 1855. Their children were: Henry, Anna, Carrie, Minnie, Walter, Alfred, William J., and Clarence. In the Spring of 1878, William decided to open his own grocery and provisions store at Frontenac Station. (The location of his store is unknown but I put him at the White Store).

By 1895, William and his family had moved to South St. Paul, Minnesota, taking his uncle, Henry Lorentzen, to live with them. According to the 1900 census, Henry Lorentzen, at the age of 79, was still living with his nephew and family in St. Paul.

John Steffenhagen Sr.

John Steffenhagen was born in Prussia in 1834. He immigrated to the United States in 1862. In 1864 he married Hannah Koch, also born in Germany, in 1833. Their children were: Florence born in 1863 and died in 1947, Wilhelmina born in 1866 and died in 1894, Amelia born in 1868 and died in 1940, Frederick born in 1870 and died in 1887 and John Jr. born in 1870 and died in 1950.

John purchased six lots from Gen. Garrard in Frontenac Station, block 5, lots 7-12 and had a house built on the corner of Germania and Italia streets. This house is presently owned by Gary Schumacher, son of Frank and Hilda (Steffenhagen) Schumacher. Hannah died in 1908. John farmed until his death in 1912. John Jr. and his wife Ella would continue to operate the farm. John was survived by two daughters, Mrs. Louis (Florence) Savage of Frontenac and Mrs. Will (Amelia) Nettleson of Eggleston and one son, John Steffenhagen Jr. residing on the farm at Frontenac.

John Steffenhagen Jr.

John Steffenhagen Jr. was born in 1871 in Minnesota, son of John and Hannah Steffenhagen. On January 4, 1909 John married Ella M. Fahje, who was also born in Minnesota, in 1888. He was engaged in farming in Florence township. Their children were Hilda M., born in 1910, Alfred W., born in 1912, Maynard Roy, born in 1921, and Hannah who died at a young age. Ella died in 1947 and John Steffenhagen, Jr. died in 1950.

John Frederick Steffenhagen

John Frederick Steffenhagen was born June 2, 1884, the son of William and Kate Steffenhagen. On December 2, 1908 John married Clara S. Kohn in Frontenac. Their children were: Dorothy, Lawrence and Robert W. By 1920 the family was living in Hastings, Minnesota. John Frederick Steffenhagen died in 1959.

John and Clara (Kohn) Steffenhagen.

Frederick Steffenhagen

Fred Steffenhagen was born in 1845 in Mecklenburg, Germany. His first wife was Caroline Heck who was also born in Germany, in 1848. In 1871 Fred, Caroline and their child immigrated to the United States, but while enroute, the child died and was buried at sea. Stopping in Chicago, Illinois for some time before arriving in Florence township, Fred and Caroline lost another baby. The Great Fire of 1871 in Chicago destroyed the cemetery and the baby's gravesite is gone. Minnie Steffenhagen was born in 1876, married Norman Sepke, moved to Canada and died in 1948. Ida Steffenhagen was born in 1878. She was an invalid for nineteen years, being blind and crippled with arthritis. She died in 1944. Louis was born in 1880 and died in 1946. Maria Johanna was born in 1881 but died the following year in 1882. In 1883, baby Fred died two days after its birth, the same day as its mother, Caroline. The two were buried together.

In 1883 Frederick married Marie Sepke who was born in Germany in 1850 and immigrated to the United States in 1880. Their children were Christopher, Carolina, Louis, Lizzy, Charles and Herman. All together, Frederick and Marie had a total of nine children. Frederick Steffenhagen died in 1930 and was survived by children: Mrs. George Santelman, Charles Steffenhagen, Herman Steffenhagen, Mrs. Carl Sepke of Florence, Mrs. Minnie Sepke and Louis Steffenhagen of Canada. Marie died in 1930. Both are buried in the Old Frontenac Cemetery.

William Steffenhagen Sr.

Born in Germany in 1852, William immigrated to America in 1874. In 1884 William and Kate Merkens were married. She was also born in Germany in 1859 and immigrated to America in 1882. After their marriage they resided many years on a farm near Frontenac Station. Their children were: Mary, John, Frieda, Elsie, William Jr., Minnie, Harvey and Carrie.

After William's death in 1909, Kate moved to Frontenac village. Katherine Steffenhagen died in 1927. Surviving her were four daughters and two sons, Mrs Ben Santelman of Frontenac, Minnie and Elsie Steffenhagen of Frontenac, Mrs. William Reiser of Kenosha, Wisconsin, William of Frontenac, and John of Hastings, Minnesota. One step-daughter, Mrs. A. R. Santelman of Frontenac also survived her. One son Harvery preceded her in death in 1925. Both William and Katherine are buried in the Old Frontenac Cemetery.

William and Caroline (Kohn) Steffenhagen.

William Steffenhagen Jr.

William Henry Steffenhagen was born in 1890 in Florence Township. In 1912, William was united in marriage to Caroline Henrietta Kohn, who was born in 1886. The marriage took place at the home of her parents at Frontenac. After their marriage, they resided on a farm near Frontenac Station. They had three children, Emery, Donald and William.

"An accident on the William Steffenhagen farm, took the life of little William "Willie" Steffenhagen, seven years old. After returning home from school, little William was riding on the wagon taking the grain from the machine to the granary. The wagon was driven by Elmer Santelman, who was hauling the last load of grain (about 70 bushels) of oats to the granary. John Lubeck's team was hitched to an

Early Residents

empty wagon and got spooked and the runaway team crashed into Santelman's wagon, throwing both him and William on the ground. The runaway team ran over little William's chest and he died.

(article in the Lake City Newspaper)

William Henry Steffenhagen died in Wabasha County in 1978 and Caroline Steffenhagen died January 15, 1971.

The Swetzer Residence ca. 1882, This postcard picture was sent to Lena (Swetzer) Earhart by her brother, Peter Swetzer Jr., saying, "Lena, this is the old house you were born in." (1912 Photo courtesy of Caroline Earhart)

The Peter Swetzer Sr. Residence 1882

This had been the home of Peter Sr. and Margarett (Witt) Swetzer, next to the Frontenac Cash Store, in the early 1880s. Their children were Henry, Willie, John, Peter Jr., and Lena. Lena was born in 1882 in this house on Columbia Street (lot 16 in block 8). Lena died in 1954 in Sacramento, California. This house was later moved to lot 5 in block 10. Later August Santelman built his house on the empty lot across from his store next to US Highway 61.

*Peter Swetzer Jr.
1877-1949*

*Lena Kate Swetzer
1882-1954*

Early Residents

Henry Webster Tackaberry 1862-1939

Henry W. Tackaberry was born in Canada and immigrated to the United States in 1880. He moved to Fargo, North Dakota. His first marriage, in 1883, was to Florence Leticia Trickey. Their children were Harry, Lester, Alice, Roy N., Dewey, and Cecil. Florence died in 1911. His second wife was "Thinka." Born in 1890, Roy Norris Tackaberry died December 30, 1918, and was buried at Arlington Cemetery, Arlington Virginia. Henry Webster Tackaberry died December 2, 1939.

The Tackaberry Brothers and Spouses, Back row, left to right: Harry, Lester, Dewey, Cecil, Front row: Charlotte, Jeanette, Alberta, Helen E. and their children. (Photo courtesy of the Tackaberry family)

Lester Charles Tackaberry 1884-1952

Lester C. Tackaberry, son of Henry and Florence Tackaberry was born in 1884 in St. Croix County, Wisconsin, and married Jeanette H. "Nettie" Scherf on July 20, 1914. They had a son, Wilbur Leroy. On January 5, 1915, Lester Tackaberry was appointed US postmaster at Frontenac Station. In 1918, Gen. Israel Garrard sold lots 4, 5, and 6 in block 8 to Charley L. Tackaberry (as he was sometimes called). By 1924 Tackaberry was working for the Milwaukee Railroad as a telegraph agent. Lester Charles Tackaberry died February 9, 1952.

Harry Percell Tackaberry 1892-1950

Harry P. Tackaberry, son of Henry and Florence Tackaberry was born in 1892. He married Charlotte A. Hahn in 1912. Their children were Richard H. and Florence. Harry was a brakeman for the railroad. He died November 8, 1950.

Early Residents

Dewey T. Tackaberry 1898-1964

Dewey Tackaberry, son of Henry and Florence Tackaberry was born in 1898 and married Alberta Schmidt. Their son, Dewey Albert Jr., was born in 1925 and died in 1992. Their family lived in Minneapolis where Dewey Sr. was a telephone operator for some time. Dewey Tackaberry died in 1964.

Cecil Cuthbert Tackaberry 1903-1956

Cecil, the son of Henry and Florence Tackaberry, was born in 1903. Cecil married his first wife, Helen E., in 1934 and they lived in Minneapolis before moving to St. Paul, where Cecil was a steward for the Great Northern Railway. By 1949 Cecil had married his second wife, Violet M. Cecil Tackaberry died in 1956.

Gilbert Terwilliger 1827-1902

Gilbert Terwilliger was born in Orange County, New York, in 1827. He married Margaret A. Sandt in 1848. She was born in 1826. In 1860 they came to this county and settled in Florence Township on a 160-acre farm in section 16, purchased from the half-breeds. He filled the office of chairman of the town board for ten years. Gilbert and Margaret's children were Elizabeth, Emma, George, Charles, Eugene, and Irvin (Ervin). Gilbert died in 1902 and Margaret died in 1915. They are buried at the Episcopal Cemetery in Frontenac.

Ervin Peter Terwilliger 1871-1952

Ervin Peter Terwilliger was the son of Gilbert and Margaret (Sandt) Terwilliger. Irvin was born in June 1871 in Florence Township. In 1895 he married Josephine Carry Roberts. Josephine was born in 1871. They farmed in Florence Township. Their children were Ruth, Myron E., Margaret, Dorothy, Robert, Florence, Gilbert W., Joseph, and Rectina.

Ervin Terwilliger, a farmer and lifelong resident of Florence Township, conducted a family orchestra for many years in Frontenac and the surrounding Red Wing area.

Josephine Carry Terwilliger died November 1, 1948. Irvin Peter Terwilliger died February 1, 1952 at the age of eighty-two. He is buried at the Episcopal Cemetery in Frontenac with his wife.

Gilbert W. Terwilliger 1904-1987

Gilbert W. Terwilliger was born January 27, 1904, at Frontenac Station, to Ervin P. and Josephine Roberts Terwilliger. He graduated from Red Wing Central High School and attended National University in Washington DC and Georgetown University. He graduated from law school in 1926. From 1931 to 1945, he served in the Minnesota State Legislature. In 1932 he was appointed to the Minnesota Bar. In 1955 he was appointed Red Wing municipal judge. He married Frances Shugrue and they had two

Early Residents

sons: James, who was born in 1936 and Ervin Peter, who was born in 1939. Frances Shugrue died in 1963. Gilbert married his second wife, June Reynolds in 1966. In 1973 he was appointed county court judge of Goodhue and Wabasha counties. He retired from his law practice in 1983. Judge Gilbert Terwilliger died in 1987 and is buried at the Frontenac Cemetery.

The Jacob and Anna (Sharpen) Witt Family

The Jacob Witt family of Hannover, Germany arrived in New York, in 1867. It was Jacob, his wife Anna (Sharpen) Witt, and two children Margaret, and Heinrich (Henry) and Henry's fiancee Katharina Lutjen. The family arrived in Florence township that same year. Jacob and Anna's second son John was born in 1869. The Witt family farmed near Central Point.

Henry Witt married Katharina (Kathy) Lutjen, in 1867. According to the 1880 census, Henry was farming in section 29, near Central Point. Jacob, and Anna were living with Henry and Kathy, helping to farm the land. Henry and Kathy's children were; Annie, John, Mary and Ida. Katharina Witt died in 1904 and Heinrich died in 1914. Both are buried in the West Florence Cemetery.

Margaret Witt married Peter Swetzer Sr. July 1867. They lived on Peter's farm in West Florence, along with Peter's father, Herman. Their five children were; Henry, William, John, Peter Jr. and Lena Kate. By 1882 Peter and Margaret had moved to Frontenac Station and rented a house next to The Frontenac Cash Store. It was in this house that Lena was born, in 1882. In 1888 the family moved to Loomis, California.

In 1896 John Witt married Carrie Tackman in West Florence. He was also farming in Florence Township. Their children were Willie born in 1900, and Edward John born in 1905. Edward later married Myrtle McKeen and operated a car repair shop at the northern end of Frontenac Station. John Witt died in 1936 and Carrie died in 1958.

Peter and Margaret (Witt) Swetzer's residence next to The Frontenac Cash Store ca. 1882. Later the August Santelman residence. (photo taken 1912, courtesy Caroline Earhart)

Early Residents

Leonard Henry Wiech

Leonard H. Wiech was born in 1922, the son of Fred and Caroline Wiech. In 1935, when Leonard was thirteen years old, he was hunting crows when his shot gun discharged and shattered his hand so badly that an amputation was necessary. Leonard's wife was Frieda Wiech. Leonard worked for Hi Park Dairy for many years. Leonard Wiech died in 2005.

The family of Johann and Eliza (Elisa) Wiech photo taken at Wells Creek c. 1900
From left to right: Amelia (Wiech) Vanberg, Annie (Wiech) Sauter - Possehl, Elisa (Hagen) Wiech, Fredrick Wiech, Johann Wiech, William Wiech, and Julius Wiech.

Anna (Wiech) Sauter-Possehl

Anna Wiech was born in Mecklenburg, Germany, in 1879, the daughter of Johann and Eliza Wiech. Anna immigrated with her parents to the United States in 1880 and settled and farmed in Hay Creek. Her siblings were: Julius, Amelia, Elize, Catarina, Frietz and William. Anna married Leo Sauter on November 14, 1906 in Red Wing. They had one son Raymond. Leo Sauter died in 1923. Anna later married Fred Possehl. Anna died in 1956. (See more information under Leo Sauter)

Early Residents

Fredrick John Wiech

Fredrick J. Wiech was born in 1891, the son of Johann and Eliza (Elisa) Wiech who immigrated to the United States from Mecklenburg, Germany, in 1880 and settled in Hay Creek. Fred married Caroline Lillian Louisa Luth, born in 1892 to John and Sophia Luth. During the 1920s and 1930s, the family was living in Florence township with their children, Arthur, George, and Leonard. Caroline had lived in the Frontenac area her entire life and was a lifelong member of St. John's Lutheran Church and was the church organist for many years, and was also a charter member of the Ladies Aid Society. Fred and Caroline divorced and Caroline later married Lawrence Miller, in 1939 in Iowa. Caroline died, in 1971 and Rev. Paul Otto officiated, with the burial at St. John's Cemetery in Lake City, Minnesota. Fred died in 1974.

Fred and Caroline Wiech with children Arthur, George and Leonard

Arthur Luth Joachim Wiech

Arthur L. Wiech was born in in 1915, the son of Fred and Caroline Wiech. In 1935 he married Lillian Freeberg in Red Wing. They had two sons, Dale and Randy. Art and Lil were the proprietors of Arts Country Club tavern from 1950 to 1961. Art died in 1973 and Lillian died in 1997. Both are buried at Oakwood Cemetery in Red Wing.

George Fredrick Wiech

George Wiech was born May 19, 1919 at Red Wing, the son of Fred and Caroline Wiech. He attended schools in the Frontenac area and later farmed for many years near Frontenac. His marriage to Dolores Stumpf took place February 27, 1939, in Wabasha. He was employed at Interstate Dock and Fuel for several years. A member of St. John's Lutheran Church, he served as church trustee and also served as supervisor of the Florence town board. George Wiech died October 28, 1967. Surviving were his wife, Dolores, two daughters, Mrs. Nile Foss of Farmington and Mrs. Matt (Jackie) Klaes of Red Wing, three sons, James of So. St. Paul, and Jerry and Jon of Frontenac; two brothers, Arthur Wiech of Frontenac and Leonard of Bloomington; his parents, Fred Wiech of Prescott and Mrs. Lawrence Miller of Frontenac.

(obit.)

Information Taken from the Goodhue County Abstract Office
(Beginning information for Frontenac Station starts in 1872)

Block #2

1872	SERVINE WEGRICK	LOT 8
1874	BLACKSMITH SHOP	LOT 10
1892	FONTENAC BUTTER & CHEESE ASSN.	LOT 13 & 14
1898	ISREAL GARRARD	LOT 13 & 14
1906	GEORGE MC MICHAEL	LOT 8
1906	ANNA WEICH	LOT 8
1911	ANNA SAUTER	LOT 8
1911	FRED & FRANCIS POSSEHL	LOT 8
1919	FRED POSSEHL	LOTS 1, 2, 3, 4, & 5
1923	CHRISTINA LARSON	LOT 9 & 10

Block #3

1881	BENJAMIN DODGE	LOT 3
1883	SEVERIN WEGRICH	LOT 16
1909	WM. PATON	LOT 14
1919	WM. PATON	LOTS 1-13

Block #4

1872	ST JOHN'S LUTHERAN CHURCH	LOT 8
1885	JOHN AKESON	LOT 3
1885	OLE ENGEBRETSON	LOT 3
1915	ST JOHN'S LUTHERAN CHURCH	LOT 1
1916	LOUISA LUTH	LOTS 1-6
1918	JOHN AKESON	1/2 OF LOT 4
1926	NORMAN MAHLER	LOT 14
1926	JOHN ALPERS	LOT 14
1929	JOHN ALPERS	LOTS 12 & 13
1873	OLE ENGEBRETSON	LOT 3
1877	WM. MAHLER	LOT 14
1885	JOHN AKESON	LOT 3
1926	JOHN ALPERS	

Block #6

1872	JAMES TOSTEVIN	LOT 7
1882	WILLIAM MUNGER	LOT 7
1882	JOHN MITCHELL	LOT 7
1882	A GUERNSEY	LOT 7
1883	JOHN MITCHEL	LOT 8
1913	BEN HOLST	LOTS 7 & 8
1921	LAURA FRANZ	LOT 7 & 8
1929	EDWARD C. WITT	LOT 1/2 OF 8
1835	WM. LUTH	LOTS 1-6
1946	CHARLEY ROPER	LOTS 7 & 8
1946	ARLAND CARLSON	LOTS 7 & 8
1950	LEONARD WEICH	LOTS 9, 10, 11, 12

Block #7

1872	DIDRICH TOPPE	LOTS 8 & 9
1878	ISAAC MUNGER	LOT 13
1881	I.G. MUNGER	LOT 14
1894	ESTATE OF ISAAC MUNGER	LOTS 13 & 14
1896-1908	MICHAEL ACKERMAN	LOTS 8 & 9
1908	JOE & MARY GERKEN	LOTS 8 & 9
1920	JULIUS SCHMIDT	LOT 1
1920	ALBERT SCHMIDT	LOTS 7 & 8
1916-1920	JULIUS SCHMIDT	LOTS 2 & 3
1920	JOE & MARY GERCKEN	LOTS 5, 6, & 7
1920	LENA MAHLER	LOT 1
1942	RICHARD GRIMM	LOTS 4, 10, 11, 12
1942	WALDO BONDE	LOTS 4, 10, 11, 12
1946	JOE & MARY GERCKEN	LOTS 8 & 9

Block #8

1873	JOHN SAUTER	LOTS 12 & 13
1873	JOHN SAUTER	LOT 5
1874	SEVERIN WEGRICH	LOT 1
1875	FRANK HAUSTEIN	LOTS 1 & 2
1878	GEORGE DODGE	LOT 16
1879	RED WING BUILDING ASSN	LOT 16
1881	JACOB SCHNEIDER	LOTS 9 & 10
1885	HERMAN SCHERF	LOT 3
1881	GEORGE H. DODGE	LOT 15
1881	JACOB SCHNEIDER	LOTS 9 & 10
1881	GEORGE DODGE	LOT 15
1882	JOHN SAUTER LOTS	12 & 13
1882	GEORGE DODGE	LOTS 12 & 13
1886	SEVERIN WEGRICH	LOT 1
1886	FRANK WEGRICH	LOT 1
1887	FRANK WEGRICH	LOT 2
1888	JOHN SAUTER	LOTS 5, 12, & 13
1902-1908	JOHN SCHMIDT	LOTS 9 & 10
1908	ALBERT SCHMIDT	LOTS 9 & 10
1916	ALBERT SCHMIDT	LOTS 7 & 8
1918	L.C. TACKABERRY	LOTS 4, 5, & 6
1918	HERMAN SCHERF TO HARRISON SCHERF	LOT 3
1926	AUGUST SANTELMAN	LOTS 1 & 2
1926	BEN SAUTER	LOTS 1 & 2
1926	GERCKEN & ACKERMAN	LOTS 11, 12, & 13
1931	KIRK HINDMAN	LOTS 11, 12, & 13
1931	EMIL & EMMA WOHLERS	LOTS 11, 12, & 13
1936	ED & MARY GERCKEN	LOTS 11, 12, & 13
1946	AUGUST SANTELMAN	LOT 15 & 16
1946	LILY ACKERMAN	LOTS 12, 13, & 14
1946	RUDOLPH & MAXINE CHARLSON	LOTS 12, 13, & 14
1947	AMBER & MARY CONRAD	LOTS 15 & 16

Block #9

1872	JOHN A. HAGER	LOT 8
1872	WM. HERLINGER	LOTS 9 & 10
1875	SEVERIN WEGRICH	LOT 7
1878	JOHN HAGER	LOT 8
1878	N. LORENTZEN	LOT 8
1881	NANCY HERLINGER	LOT 11
1886	FRANCIS SAUTER	LOT 7
1887	JOHN B. SAUTER	LOT 5
1887	H. LORENTZEN	LOT 8
1887	FREDRICK LORENTZEN & H. LORENTZEN	LOT 8
1888	JOHN SAUTER	LOT 5 & PT 6
1887	JOHN HAGER	LOTS 5 & 6
1887	JOHN B. SAUTER	LOT 5 & 6
1888	JOHN SAUTER (WIDOWER) TO DAUGHTER VICTORIA SAUTER	LOT 7
1888	AUGUST SAUTER	LOT 5
1890	FREDRICK LORENTZEN TO H. LORENTZEN	LOT 8
1893	JOHN HAGER	LOT 8
1905	NANCY HERLINGER	LOTS 9 & 10 & 11
1905	WM STEFFENHAGEN	LOTS 9 & 10
1906	ESTATE OF JOHN HAGER TO HJERMSTAD & SANTELMAN	LOTS 5 & 6
1910	AUGUST & MARY SANTELMAN	LOTS 9, 10, & 11
1910	JOHN & FRIEDA STEFFENHAGEN	LOTS 9, 10 & 11
1914	A.W. FICK	LOTS 13 & 14
1919	STATE BANK TO ANTON SCHAFER, FRED WOHLERS & JOHN ALPERS	LOTS 12 & 13 (PARTIAL)
1919	JOHN DAMMAN	LOTS 13 & 14
1919	JOHN DAMMAN	LOTS 1, 2, 3, & 4
1921	WM. STEFFENHAGEN	LOTS 9, 10, & 11
1921	HJERMSTAD & SANTELMAN	LOTS 5 & 6
1921	AUGUST & MARY SANTELMAN	LOTS 5, 6, & 7
1921	LEO & ANNIE SAUTER	LOTS 5, 6 & 7
1922	LOUIS & ED PETERS	LOTS 5, 6, & PART OF LOT 7
1923	LEO SAUTER	LOTS 5, 6, & 7
1923	BEN SAUTER	LOTS 5, 6, & 7
1925	LOUIS PETERS	LOTS 5, 6, & 7
1925	EDWARD F. PETERS	LOTS 5, 6, & 7
1927	JOHN DAMMAN	LOTS 1, 2, 3, & 4
1927	ERNEST ALPERS	LOTS 1, 2, 3, & 4
1928	NANCY HERLINGER	LOTS 9 & 10
1928	GRACE WEICH	LOTS 9, 10 & 11
1928	GRACE WIECH	LOTS 1, 2, 3, & 4
1931	KIRK & AMY HINDMAN	LOTS 12 & 13
1931	WM. & GRACE WIECH	LOTS 12 & 13
1935	JOHN DAMMAN	LOTS PART OF 13 & ALL OF 14
1935	MINNIE GABE	LOTS PART OF 13 & ALL OF 14
1936	S. A. & MABEL RICE	LOTS 1, 2, 3, & 4

Block #10

1885	LOUIS & ELIZABETH KLOCKE	LOT 7
1885	CARL AUGUST PETERS	LOT 7 (SINGLE)
1889	JOACHIM PETERS	LOT 7
1920	GEORGE GARRARD	LOT 6
1920	JOE PETERS	LOT 6
1920	GEORGE GARRARD	LOT 5
1920	JOHN DAMMAN	LOT 5
1930	H. L. & ANNA HJERMSTAD	LOT 5
1932-1936	HERMAN & SUSSIE D. KUHFUSS	LOT 10
1936	J.W. REICHERT	LOT 10
1939	ATHEL HULVORSON	LOT 10
1944	FRED & CECILE REICHERT	LOT 10
1944	ATHEL HULVORSON	LOT 10
1946-1948	M. L. PRIEBE	LOT 10
1947	EDWIN HUNEKE	LOT 4
1948	FRANCIS SHEPHARD	LOT 10
1948	LOUIS & VIRGIL RIDGEWAY	LOT 10 (FATHER & SON)
1950	VIRGIL RIDGEWAY	LOT 10 (SON DECEASED)
1950	LOUIS & MARY RIDGEWAY	LOT 10 (HUSBAND & WIFE)
1956	EDWIN SELCK	LOT 10
1957	CARL BLAKELY	LOT 10
1957	ROBERT & PEARL LEHMAN	LOT 10

Block #11

1871	ISRAEL GARRARD	LOT 11
1872	NICHOLAS KREST	LOT 11
1873	JACOB SCHNEIDER	LOT 12
1886	ALEXANDER CAMERON	LOT 12
1887	JOHN SCHMIDT	LOT 12
1895	ALBERT SCHMIDT	LOT 12
1895	JOHN SCHMIDT	LOTS 1 & 2
1895	C.E. FRIEDRICH	LOTS 1 & 2
1895	C.E. FRIEDRICH	LOT 12
1910	LUDWIG HEINE	LOTS 9 & 10
1910	FRANK BUSCH	LOTS 9 & 10
1910	JAMES A. SMITH LUMBER CO.	LOT 9 & 10
1913	B.C. & LENA FRENCH	LOT 11
1914	GRACE HEINE	LOTS 9 & 10
1915	LEO SAUTER	LOTS 9 & 10
1916	LEO & ANNA SAUTER	LOT 11
1918	LEO & ANNA SAUTER	LOTS 7 & 8
1922	ALBERT & BERTHA SCHMIDT	LOT 12
1923	LEO & ANNA SAUTER	LOT 12
1923	LEO & ANNA SAUTER	LOTS 1, 2, 7, 8, 9,10 & 12
1926	GEORGE GARRARD	LOTS 1-6
1927	ANNA SAUTER POSSEHL RAYMOND A. SAUTER/WM SCHERF	LOTS 1-6

Goodhue County Abstract Information

Block #12

1872	ISRAEL GARRARD	LOTS 1 & 2
1872	JACOB & BARBARA SCHNEIDER	LOTS 1 & 2
1892	E. A. KEMPE	LOTS 1 & 2
1894	BARBARA SCHNEIDER	LOTS 1 & 2
1894	C. E. FREIDRICH	LOTS 1 &2
1895	ALBERT SCHMIDT	LOTS 1 &2
1923	LEO SAUTER	LOTS 1 & 2
1925	ANNA & SON RAYMOND SAUTER	LOTS 1 & 2
1928	GEORGE GARRARD	LOT 6
1928	WILLIAM SCHERF	LOT 6
1932	CHARLES J. LEMKE	LOTS 3 & 4
1941	VIRGIL & VIOLET MARTINSON	LOTS 3 & 4
1944	ANNA (MOTHER) & RAY (SON) SAUTER	LOTS 1 & 2
1949	VIRGIL & VIOLET MARTINSON	LOTS 1, 2, 3, 4
1949	WALDO BONDE	LOTS 1, 2, 3, 4

Block #13

ISRAEL GARRARD

Block #14

1874	ISRAEL GARRARD	LOTS 5 & 6
1874	JOSEPH BEST & JAMES TOSTEVIN	LOTS 5 & 6
1875	TOSTEVIN JR.	LOTS 5 & 6
1875	H. LORENTZEN	LOTS 5 & 6
1878	ISRAEL GARRARD	LOT 4
1878-1912	NILS & ELLEN CARSTENSON	LOT 4
1881	JAMES TOSTEVIN	LOTS 5 & 6
1883	N. LORENTZEN	LOTS 5 & 6
1883	JOHN MITCHELL & ANDREW EATON	LOTS 5 & 6
1887	JAMES RALSTON	LOTS 5 & 6
1889	NILS CARSTENSON	LOT 4
1912-1923	BENJAMIN HOLST	LOT 4
1923	ROBERT & LAURA FRANZ	LOT 4
1923	ISABELLE McKEEN	LOT 4

The Village of Florence

In 1858 the village of Florence was platted south of Frontenac Station along Lake Pepin. A post office was established in 1858 and was in operation until 1867. The small farming village had one store and a school. Much of the plat was never developed and it was abandoned in 1886 and 1929.

(Goodhue County Historical News, "Florence Township")

A. M. C. Johnston, who settled in Florence Township in 1856, was one of the first settlers of Florence village, along with other early settlers D. H. and E. M. Vining, J. C. Munger, D. T. Weed, M. C. Kelly, and O. P. Francisco. Aaron Hudson had the only store in Florence, with John Kelly as the justice of the peace.

News Briefs from the Village of Florence

D. H. Vining sold to G. T. Reynolds, 320 acres of land in section 23, Florence, for a consideration of $6,800.

(1887)

D. H. Vining was one of the pioneer settlers in Florence, having lived there from 1855 to 1876. He died in 1894, at his home in Lake City, at the age of seventy-six.

Oscar Vining of Florence was gored by a bull and is now recovering.

(1885 Advance Sun)

Funeral services were held for Isaac G. Munger in 1893. Munger was born in Michigan in 1834 and was fifty-nine years old at the time of his death. In 1864 he came to Minnesota and located in the town of Florence. He was an agent for several different elevator companies. At the time of his death, he was buying grain for G. D. Post of Lake City.

John Sauter, an old resident of Florence, has decided to move to St. Paul.

(1888)

Jacob Brock, living in the town of Florence, has five children sick with diphtheria and John Thompson has one child sick with the same disease.

(1887)

Two Sunday schools of Florence unite in a picnic near John B. Schafer and Andrew Eaton's farms.

(1887)

The ladies of Florence belonged to "The Needlecraft Neighbors" which was formerly the "Florence Club" in 1906.

Emmanuel Schenach was a wagonmaker in the town of Florence in 1870. His wife's name was Starel and their children were Jose, Victoria, and John.

Gottfried Schenach was a blacksmith at Florence. His wife's name was Annie and their children were Ariel, Engelbert, and Joseph.

George Burmeister was a miller.

The Village of Florence

Pleasant Valley
Florence Township

In the 1850s, the territorial road was the only land route between St. Paul and "civilization" in Dubuque, Iowa. A part of that original road, now called Ski Road, ran through a small community that included a dozen homes, District 25 School, an abandoned township road that ran west to the top of the bluffs, and an earth and limestone dam across one of the larger coulees. According to the old plat books, this area went dormant sometime during the Great Depression.

Most of the land has been purchased by the Minnesota Department of Natural Resources (DNR). North of Ski Road is now the Perched Valley WMA, (Wildlife Management Association) and south of the road is part of the Richard J. Dorer State Hardwood Forest. Two home sites still exist along the old territorial road (Ashbaugh & Oley), and one on the old township road (Murphy). Two wooden structures with block foundations were demolished by the DNR about 1989. Four limestone and one poured concrete foundation can still be found along the wooded creek beds.

The foundations of the District 25 School still exist. Its access road, across from the old township road, has long since filled in with trees and shrubs, but every spring the perennial flowers, planted back then, still bloom.

Several large steep coulees were formed in the bluffs and the largest, east-west running coulee was dammed up with an earthen dam and used as a small mill. The pond that formed behind it was twelve feet deep, thirty yards wide, and fifty yards long. The two-foot diameter overflow pipe that ran underneath to the creek is unmistakably from the Red Wing Sewer Pipe Company. Limestone and concrete walls were set into the center of the dam to form a race and mill. Sediment, washed from the bluffland fields above, settled to the bottom. At some point, there were fish—and fishermen—in the pond, as evidenced by old hooks, lures, sinkers, and painted cork bobbers (no plastic) recovered from the thick loam that now fills the coulee.

Over the years various millsets could have been used, including a barrel slat grinder for making of apple mash, the main ingredient of apple vinegar. Since there was no refrigeration, food was preserved by drying, salting, canning, or pickling. Pickling required vinegar. Many apple orchards were planted around the area. There were eating apples, baking apples, cider apples, and the rest were probably sent to this mill for apple mash.

Sometime in the 1920s, this earthen dam was opened, and a new creek bed cut through the pond bottom. Many of the dam's limestone reinforcing blocks remain.

According to the old plat books, Florence Township maintained a township road that started on the Territorial Road (Ski Road) across from School District 25, and went up to the top of the bluff, connecting with Circle S Road, near the present Boldt farm. A bridge across one of the side ravines was made with old riveted iron railroad trestle sides, and big oak timbers cut from surrounding trees. Winter snowmelt and rains on the steep bluffs took their toll on this road, however. The bridge supports washed out and were replaced with culverts. Several other washouts forced this road to be abandoned circa 1940. The DNR presently maintains a logging and snowmobile trail on the southern side of these coulees.

(Compiled and written by Michael Murphy)

Florence Township Schools

Frontenac School
District #24

(Photo courtesy of Ellen Stewart)

Organized in 1857, a schoolhouse was erected in Old Frontenac on land donated by Israel Garrard. This typical one-room school also held services of the Episcopal Church until their church was built. After the Chicago, Milwaukee & St. Paul Railroad line was completed through Frontenac Station, the schoolhouse, which consisted of the eight elementary grades, was moved to a location half-way between the two Frontenac villages. According to Clarence Peterson, interviewed by Alverna Miller in 1999, the school used to be on "Preachers Row" in Old Frontenac. They tried to move it to New Frontenac, but the schoolhouse was too large to move across the narrow bridge that was over the swamp at that time. The school was then sited between the villages, where the move had to end.

For several years, this school was the only school in the county which had a belfry with a bell attached.

In 1955 the district consolidated with the Lake City Public School. The Frontenac School would be used for grades 1, 2 and 3, only, and the other children were bused to the public school in Lake City. This one-room schoolhouse saw almost one hundred years of classes come and go.

The era of rural school education in Goodhue County ended in the 1950s—due to consolidations. Two schools remained open longer, one in the Belvidere area, for a short time, and the other, in Welch, District 167, which closed in the late 1960s.

Florence Township Schools - 24, 25, 26, and 27

Inside the classroom of School District #24 ca. 1930

Students of School District #24 ca. 1930 (Photo courtesy of Jean Dankers)

Florence Township Schools - 24, 25, 26, and 27

J. F. Terry was teaching school at Frontenac for several months in 1889, while Thomas Lutz opened for the fall term at Frontenac in 1889. Miss Amy Stone had been re-elected principal of the Frontenac graded school, according to the Advance Sun in 1891.

"H. W. Keller, who is teaching the Frontenac school this year, removed his family to that burgh Saturday. He has purchased a residence from General Garrard. During his stay here Prof. Keller taught the school in our village (Hay Creek) fifteen terms, a record that is equaled by few if any of the teachers in the country schools of this county."

(Oct. 8, 1895 Daily Republican)

School District 24 opened in 1901, with an enrollment of sixty-one scholars. Various teachers over the years were: Emma Schenach in 1907, Miss Cane in 1910, Miss Louise Sauter in 1912, Anna Gessner of Plainview from 1914-1917, Julia Anderson in 1918 and Miss Mabel Joseph of Red Wing in 1919, Beth Furst taught in 1920, and Helen Jansen had been the principal in 1922. Mary Reinhard of Lake City was the teacher for the upper grades from 1935-1937, and Miss Lucille Thompson taught the lower grades. Lyrene Heins taught in 1938 with Dorothy Fick teaching from 1938-1941 with Alma Bremer also teaching from 1939-1940. Josephine Stone taught from 1941-1942 and Laura Dethloff from 1943-1945. Irene Cronin taught from 1946-1947, Rose Eichhorn in 1948 and Grace Kuhl from 1949-1954.

(From History of Goodhue County Rural Schools GCHS)

Postcard photograph of Frontenac students in Miss Louise Sauter's class. (GCHS)

Florence Township Schools - 24, 25, 26, and 27

In 1912 Miss Louise Sauter closed a very successful nine months term of school in District #24 on Friday June 7, 1912. On Saturday evening the pupils rendered their closing program at the town hall. An excellent program was rendered in which each and every one carried out their parts admirably well. County Superintendent, Swain was also present and delivered an address on "Education, Morally and Intellectually." He also presented the diplomas to the graduates of the 8th grade, who were: Nathaniel Peterson, Gerald Clifford, George Akeson, Carl Akeson and Carl Larson. The Frontenac Star Band rendered some excellent selections. After the program, the young folks enjoyed dancing for several hours.
(1912)

Hilda (Steffenhagen) Schumacher's class at District 24 School (Photo courtesy of Gary Schumacher)

School News

Frontenac was the first district to make return of the adoption of the free text book system.
(1889 Republican)

The Florence schoolhouse was broken into one night last week, and vandals despoiled the room, very similar to the destruction at the Frontenac schoolhouse, earlier.
(1891 Advance Sun)

Thorwald Carstenson, Ole Evenson, and A. Baas, who broke into the Frontenac school house last December and committed various act of vandalism, pleaded guilty Tuesday in court, to an indictment charging them with malicious destruction of property. They were each fined one dollar and one third of the costs, which amount to a considerable item. It is said there are three indictments yet to be made public.
(1892 Advance Sun)

Florence Township Schools - 24, 25, 26, and 27

Pleasant Valley School
District #25

(Photo courtesy of GCHS)

The Pleasant Valley School (District 25) was organized in 1857, with the building being erected in 1892 on the corner of a one-acre plot near the Lewis Orchard. It was located on the south side of the marsh of Simmons Creek, which flows through Lidberg Pond, and along the old military road between Wacouta and Frontenac. The foundation and well are still visible and the perennial flowers, planted many years ago near the school, still bloom every summer.

In 1894 Miss Josephine Roberts taught at District 25 with Stella VanGuilder teaching in 1917, Jean Masterson in 1919 and Mrs. H. Masterson teaching from 1920-1921. Harriet Jansen taught in 1922, Eleanor Oelkers from 1935-1938, Grace Kuhl from 1939-1940, Joyce Carlson in 1941, Mariagne Anderson in 1942, Mrs. Kells from 1943-1947, and Margaren Isensee from 1948-1949. Evelyn Wendler Nelson did her practice teaching here with Mamie (Magme) Peterson Snow. The school closed in 1950.

(History of Goodhue County Rural Schools courtesy of GCHS)

Florence Township Schools - 24, 25, 26, and 27

Sunnyside School
District #26

(Photo courtesy of GCHS)

Organized in 1862, this school building was erected in 1893 near the site of the old Union Mill, on the corner of William Hahn's land, which adjoined Julius Schmidt's land and also adjoined land owned by Gilbert Terwilliger.

Some of the various teachers and the years they taught were: in 1894, Miss Lizzie C. Mitchell, in 1916, Maude [Maud] Schmidt taught, Sadie Newton in 1917, Mabel E. Nelson in 1918, Ruth Olson in 1920, Ethel Ennis in 1921, Charlotte Wolfmeyer in 1922, Miss Evelyn Samuelson in 1929, Ione Truedson in 1935, Geneva Longren in 1936, Grace Kuhl from 1937-1938, Hilda Carlson from 1939-1940, Grace Kuhl from 1941-1948, Agnes Tushaus from 1949-1951, Helen Steffenhagen from 1952-1953, Blanche Ovalson in 1954 and Luella Carlson in 1955. In 1956 they consolidated with Red Wing.

(History of Goodhue County Rural Schools courtesy of GCHS)

Florence Township Schools - 24, 25, 26, and 27

Florence School
District #27

Organized about 1863, the building was erected in 1867 and was located in the village of Florence, east of Frontenac Station and Wells Creek. (Photo courtesy of GCHS)

Carpenter School

In November 1893, the new school house in Florence Township was formally dedicated. Rev. John Watson of Lake City delivered an address. This one-room schoolhouse was built on the left side of Staehli Park Road, close to the railroad tracks. When trains passed, class was stopped, as students were unable to hear the teacher. The teachers roomed and boarded with the Nelson family along Highway 61. Students carried drinking water from the Falkner farm, located across the road from the school.

(Info from the Friends of the Florence Town Hall Newsletter)

Last Friday evening, a large number of people gathered at the Carpenter School House in the town of "Florence" to show Mr. E. F. Carpenter their appreciation of him and his family. Edwin Wrigley toasted Carpenter and spoke of their friendship. Rev. John Watson was also there and gave a speech. Mr. Carpenter sold his farm and was moving to Tennessee.

(1894 Advance Sun)

In 1917 Madge Merrill taught school and Avis Hyslop in 1918, Helen Dennen in 1921, Rectina Terwilliger in 1935, Marguerite Dahl from 1936-1938, Clara Pederson from 1939-1940, Evelyn Thompson in 1941, Dorothy Fick in 1942, Mary Posz in 1943, Mrs. Cronin in 1944, Leah C. Sass from 1945-1946, and Laura Cuffel from 1947-1949. They were closed by 1950 and consolidated with Lake City in 1955.

When the school closed in 1949, the building was moved to the Washington Schoolyard in Lake City to be used as a gym until a new school was built. Later it was sold at an auction to a farmer who used it for a shed.

(Photo courtesy of Marcia Savela)

Bramble Haw

On US Highway 61, about one mile southeast of Frontenac Station, you will notice state forest land. At one time, this had been the home of Col. and Mrs. James Munro. Originally from the East, the Munros loved the beauty of the Frontenac area and purchased one hundred and sixty acres of land. In 1925 they built a New England-style cottage on this land. They called their property Bramble Haw, which actually meant "prickly hawthorn bush."

In 1929 Col. Munro died. During this time Lulu Munro's sister, Nell Mabey, was working as the women's page editor for the Minneapolis Tribune. After the colonel's death, Nell decided to give up her job at the Tribune, and moved to Bramble Haw, to live with her sister.

Lulu Munro died in 1953. Before their deaths, James and Lulu Munro had stated that they wanted their estate to be preserved. In 1954 Lulu's sister, Nell Mabey, was instrumental in establishing the Frontenac State Park Association, which was the beginning of Frontenac State Park, on the one hundred sixty acres of Bramble Haw.

The Munros house served as the state park manager's residence for some time, but unfortunately, was torn down in 1990. Now, all that is left to remind people of this once beautiful estate just a few feet off US State Highway 61 is the entrance to Frontenac State Park, with its stone wall and iron gate, once the entrance to Bramble Haw.

(Photo courtesy of Marcia Savela)

Nell Mabey

Nell Mabey was born September 2, 1874, in Long Prairie, Minnesota, to Joseph and Lucinda Mabey. By 1880 the family had moved to Lake City, Minnesota, where Nell spent much of her youth. In 1894 Nell got her education at the University of Minnesota and in 1910 she moved to Minneapolis, where she started her career as the women's page editor for the Minneapolis Tribune. This career would last twenty-five years.

Nell's brother-in-law, Col. James Munro, died in 1929 and shortly after, Nell gave up her career with the Tribune, and went to live with her sister, Lulu Munro, at Bramble Haw. It was there that Nell Mabey started to write poetry. Inspired as she walked through the woods and worked in the garden alongside her favorite companion, her dog, Whimpie, an Irish Water Spaniel, her poetry started to flow. In 1938 her collection of poetry, Clover Blooms, came out and in 1955 Nell's book, Whimpie of Bramble Haw, was written about her lovable dog.

When Nell's sister, Lulu, died in 1953, Nell stayed on at Bramble Haw for a short time before moving to Lake City. She was a charter member of the Lake City Women's Club, and also belonged to the Lake City Old Settlers Association, the Frontenac State Park Association, and the Minnesota Poets League. Nell Mabey is now considered one of Minnesota's very well-known women's poets. Nell died in Lake City on June 30, 1959, and is buried at Lakewood Cemetery in Lake City.

Artist drawing of Bramble Haw. (Photo courtesy of Marcia Savela)

The stone wall and iron gate, the only reminders of the entrance to Bramble Haw. (Photo courtesy of Marcia Savela)

Lake City Airport

History of the Lake City and Frontenac Municipal Airport

From November 1933, when the Lake City Council moved to build an airport with federal grant monies and approved a land donation of one dollar per year from R. D. Underwood, president of Jewell Nursery Company, the airport operated as a public airfield. This annual donation continued until the early 1960s. During these thirty-plus years much activity surrounded the building of the airport from a private airfield to an emergency landing field to a potential feeder airport for domestic long distance flights.

Early History of the Underwood Airport

In February 1931, E. B. Freeman, formerly from Lake City, representing Freeman Aircraft Sales, an authorized agent for Stinson Aircraft, Minneapolis, visited the Underwood private airfield in the Frontenac Station area. The purpose of the trip was to look at developing the airfield into a public airfield, specifically looking at the approaches to the field. The field was at that time operated privately by the Jewell Nursery Company.

Directions to get to the Florence Township airstrip at that time was by taking Highway 3 pavement to the Young farm and then driving past the Ryan farm.

(Compiled and written in 2007 by Andru M. Peters, Lake City, Minnesota, and submitted by the Lake City Historical Society)

Early Beginnings of the Lake City Airport

The final plans were approved for the development of a new airfield on December 13, 1933. With the approval of constructing an airfield, this would create a first-class airport. Construction work started in December 1933 with the land being graded, leveled, drained, and marked for two identified runways with landing lights. At the same time a third runway was approved to be added. The Civil Works Program airport project commenced work in December 1933 with seventy-seven Wabasha county workers who were used for clearing brush, cutting trees, and grubbing.

In 1932 Northwest Airways Inc. had also designated the airfield as an emergency landing field.

In 1935 Frontenac landowners in the vicinity of the airport signed petitions to secure a change in the location of the road, which limited the length of the north and south runways. The Department of Commerce issued new rulings on runway lengths, which meant that the road needed to be moved seven-tenths of a mile.

Growth of the Lake City Airport-1940s

In January 1940 the Lake City Airport was awarded by the Civil Aeronautics Authority the emergency landing airfield for aircraft status. The mowed grass airfield had an east-west runway of 4,400 feet and a north-south runway of 2,500 feet.

The official name assigned to the newly designated air field was Frontenac Field, Site 28-B, and had a radio signal "G" assigned which was on the Chicago-Twin Cities flight path. The field was designed to send out weather reports of the conditions around the field every thirty-five minutes. The field also launched weather balloons into the clouds to calculate the altitude of the clouds. The field at that time was manned "24/7" by attendants W. V. Hixon, R. C. Fevre, Roy L. Messmore and J. C. MacAdam.

The Frontenac airfield during the year 1940 was called one of the best emergency landing fields in the country. This airport replaced a much smaller field located in Hager City, Wisconsin. The change was due to the fact that the Hager City field was too small for large planes.

By 1941 the airfield had built an office, communications building, storage shed, and a beacon tower. Also housed at the airfield was Vince Brown, Minneapolis owner of Ace Flying School.

On December 11, 1941, shortly after the start of World War II, the airport was closed to the public except those on official business. The move was in response to action taken as a precaution against sabotage with the beginning of the war with Japan. In 1942 a group of civilian spotters were organized. These spotters were mostly local women between the ages of nineteen and thirty-five. Each township would have a minimum of ten observers working in pairs comprised of a chief spotter and an alternate spotter.

In September 1944 the Civil Aeronautics Administration made a presentation to the Lake City Chamber of Commerce. The plan was for the city to take over the airport with the CAA agreeing to maintain the weather bureau and the communication station on the field. Jack Lowrie of Lake City, who had a flying school with two hangars located next to the field, offered to take over the commercial privileges of the airport. The new plan called for tearing down the two small hangars and replace these buildings with a larger hangar built of cement blocks, 160 by 140 feet, which is still standing today.

Airport Dedication

On October 7, 1945, the dedication of the Lake City airport was made on the site of the former Frontenac airport. John "Jack" Lowrie sub-leased the site from the City of Lake City for the airport and had built a hangar, repair shop, restaurant, and administration building. Also on site was the Civil Aeronautics Communication station complete with radio equipment, weather observatory, and radio and teletype connection with other flying fields. The field, at dedication time, had three runways, which included a north-south runway of 2,470 feet, a northwest-southeast runway of 4,420 feet, and an east-west runway of 3,000 feet. Thousands of people attended the grand opening event.

The airfield was to be considered the headquarters for a major airline (most likely Northwest Airlines), with flights from Lake City to Chicago and the West Coast.

In 1946 a plane used in the Normandy invasion was purchased and Mr. Bartsh and Jack Vogle operated charter flights out of the Lake City-Frontenac airport.

During the week of April 15, 1946, the Lake City airport along with the airport at Hager City, Wisconsin, were designated by the War Department as GI training centers for former servicemen, providing free flight training for all enrolled war veterans. It was projected that up to one thousand men would be trained at these airfields.

The fields were to be operated by Mid-Cities Aviation Company, which Jack Lowrie owned. It was expected that with this contract the airport would add additional hangar and shop buildings, as well as a coffee shop.

By 1947 Minnesota had 190 landing fields. Early projections for the Lake City-Frontenac airfield was to average fifteen tourists using the field each day. During March 1947, members of the Lake City Chamber Airport Committee went to St. Paul to petition for the continuance of the airport located in Frontenac.

In an attempt to keep the airport operations going and to expand the current operations, on May 9, 1947, the Red Wing City Council rejected a proposal for a joint airport operation in Frontenac with Lake City. The Red Wing Council then approved $104,000 for improvements to the Hager City, Wisconsin, airport. The reasons for rejecting the joint proposal was that the Frontenac airport was too far from Red Wing and the "dangerous" railroad crossing caused concerns amongst the projected users of the airport.

The beginning of the end of airport operations occurred in September 1948 when a new gravel washing plant was built next to the airport. The plant was located on the west side of the landing strip and is currently located there.

Lake City Airport

Prior to 1946, the airport at Frontenac provided an emergency landing spot for commercial traffic flying overhead. The airway connected Minneapolis and St. Paul with Chicago, with scheduled stops in Winona, La Crosse, and Madison.

The old airport was also a government-certified airport and civil aeronautics station. During the war, the airport staff watched for enemy aircraft. That was the reason the government was helping to get smaller airports started. The airport at Frontenac had an aircraft repair station, weather station, and a lunch counter. Joseph McAdams was the radio station operator at the airport in 1940.

By the mid-1940s, the government did not see the need for auxiliary airports for the airlines and closed the airport.

(Taken from Republican Eagle *November 26 & 27, 2011)*

Jack and Flora Lowrie sub-leased the airport in the 1940s from the City of Lake City and opened a flight school. The building and runway were already there, but the Lowries remodeled the hangar and added an office. They also added a restaurant, so people from out of town would have a place to eat. Most of their clients had private planes based at the Frontenac Airport. For convenience, restaurants in town provided transportation for these clients.

Mid-City Aviation Company was geared to serving American veterans and offered sightseeing rides and pilot instruction. They trained many pilots in Piper Cubs and other aircraft.

Jack and Flora had three small two-seater planes and one big four-seater. The couple hired three pilots as instructors. Harold "Schmitty" Schmidt was one of them.

After World War II they started a school for veterans. A lot of veterans learned to fly on the GI bill. In those days some farmers had ultralights and small airstrips on their farms, and would fly from their farms. They could carry one or two people like a regular plane, but they were open, with just seats.

Jack and Schmitty would pick up students on their farms in the morning and take them home at night. The airport was strictly for daytime flying as there were no lights on the runway.

The Lowries had the airport until 1947. By that time, Mid-City Aviation Company was flying passengers round-trip from Lake City to California, Florida, New Orleans, and St. Louis.

(Story by Ginger Holm as told by Katie Schmidt and Flora Lowrie)

Lake City Airport

Airport Station Closed to Public

In 1941 orders to restrict entry to the Frontenac Communications Station CAA airport and weather station, were received at the airport. The order stated that all facilities of the station were closed to the public except persons on official business or well known to the operator.

"No admittance" signs were posted at the weather observatory and communication building. The move was in line with action taken throughout the United States as a precaution against sabotage since the beginning of the war with Japan.

Anyone prowling around the station or molesting property would do so at their own risk. To enforce this, the soldiers from company E of Red Wing stood guard 24 hours a day at the Frontenac airport.

(1941 Lake City Graphic)

In 1947 a new emergency airport was built eleven miles from Red Wing at Frontenac Station, under the WPA (Works Progress Administration) program. The Frontenac field covered 115 acres and the lease provided for an annual rental payment of $1,150 at the rate of ten dollars an acre. The airport that was already there had sufficient space on the field for an east-west runway about a mile long and a north-south runway about three-quarters of a mile in length.

Dr. Eugene Jonas starting his plane at the Lake City Airport. (Photos courtesy of Syvilla Bloom)

Lake City Airport/Nimon-Cushing Airport

Romaine Nimon was an instructor at the government supported Mid-City Airport (Lake City/Red Wing Airport) near Frontenac Station. Bob Cushing took his first flying lesson on September 17, 1944. Seven months later, he earned his commercial license and flight instructor certification. He then began instructing with Nimon for Jack Lowrie at Mid-City Airport in March 1946.

In the spring of 1945 the Red Wing City Council voted $3,000 for an airport survey. The survey was taken and the site recommended by the Wisconsin Planning Commission was in Trenton Township, off Highway 35, across the Mississippi River from Red Wing. In September 1945, the State of Minnesota allotted $25,000 for a Red Wing Airport project with a flying strip, an equal amount of matching funds to be provided by the city.

On January 24, 1946, Romaine Nimon and Bob Cushing received permission from L. J. Moes to use a parcel of his land, overlooking Goose Lake near Bay City, Wisconsin, as a landing field and airport. This was to be a forerunner to the present Red Wing Airport near Bay City, Wisconsin. By late spring, the Nimon-Cushing field was operational and most of Bob Cushing's flying would continue out of this field for the next few years.

Romaine and Cushing were flying for Mid-City and, as local young men returned from the service with their GI Bills in hand, flight instruction flourished. The Nimon-Cushing field would instruct the overflow that could not be handled at Mid-City.

After the war, when the federal government began to withdraw supporting funds from Mid-City Airport in Frontenac and other small airports around the country, and when it was learned that local funding may be available, Nimon and Cushing approached the boards at Lake City and Red Wing. They suggested that the cities continue leasing the acreage at Frontenac from the area farmers to keep the airport in existence and, in return, they would help run it and continue to give instruction. Lake City and Red Wing declined.

In 1946 the City of Red Wing purchased the recommended 120 acres of land in Isabelle Township, graded a runway and access road and installed a windsock. William Pierce, member of the aviation board told Alderman Betcher that the proposed airfield is a "purely business proposition and not a playground for soldiers coming back, although its use will be available to them."

Following the end of the war, the number of returning servicemen was reduced to a trickle and business at the Goose Lake field tailed off dramatically. With little money coming in and unable to support their flying operations, increasing competition from the improving Red Wing facility forced the Nimon-Cushing Field to close in late 1948.

(Submitted by Vance Cushing, son of Bob Cushing)

Lake City Airport

Unidentified pilot coming out of the door of the Airport Inn, the restaurant that was located within the Lake City Airport. "Charley" was written on the back of the picture. (Photo courtesy of Syvilla Bloom)

Two unidentified men, most likely a pilot and mechanic, standing next to the Lake City Airport building in the early 1950s. (Photo courtesy of Syvilla Bloom)

Small plane landing at the Lake City Airport.

Windsock and landing field at the Lake City Airport.

Unidentified pilot and his plane on the airfield at the Lake City Airport.

Unidentified pilot and his plane on the airfield at the Lake City Airport.

Lake City Airport

New Spring Flying Courses
STARTING NOW

FOR INFORMATION SEE

Bob Cushing	Romaine Nimon
Nimon-Cushing Field 2 Miles East of Hager City	Lake City Airport at Frontenac

Mid-Cities Aviation School
FRONTENAC, MINN

Will Begin a Ground School Frontenac—Nov. 27th

It will include a complete course of instruction leading to a private pilot's license. The price of the instruction to each individual will be $20.00 and this will include the books and other required equipment. Instruction in meteorology, navigation, civil aeronautics, traffic rules and care and operation of aircraft will be taken up in enough detail to permit the student to pass a private pilot's examination.

Anyone Interested Is Invited to Attend the First Meeting Scheduled at
Shep's Tavern
8:30 P. M. MONDAY, NOV. 27TH
FRONTENAC, MINN.

At this meeting the details will be discussed and those interested will be registered for the course.

1944

LEARN TO FLY
See Us About Instructions For Information

at NIMON-CUSHING FIELD	at LAKE CITY AIRPORT
Bob Cushing Taylor Bunch	Romaine Nimon Perry Goodsell

MID-CITIES AVIATION

1946

Dedication..
LAKE CITY AIRPORT
Frontenac, Minnesota

SUNDAY, OCT. 7, 1945

Free Entertainment All Day
Food and Soft Drinks at Field
Flying Course Given Away
Tickets for Rides May Be Purchased at Field All During the Day

1945

Airplane flights will be made during entire day from Underwood Air Field, Located Only Two Miles West of Lake City. New Stinson Four Passenger Cabin Plane, Piloted by E. J. Fowler, Pilot for Freeman Aircraft Sales, With 3,000 Flying Hours.

225